Bedfordshire, Buckinghamshire and Hertfordshire

NICK CORBLE

COUNTRYSIDE BOOKS
NEWBURY BERKSHIRE

Contents

Contents

WALKS IN HERTFORDSHIRE

PUBLISHER'S NOTE

We hope that you obtain considerable enjoyment from this book; great care has been taken in its preparation. Although at the time of publication all routes followed public rights of way or permitted paths, diversion orders can be made and permissions withdrawn.

We cannot, of course, be held responsible for such diversion orders and any inaccuracies in the text which result from these or any other changes to the routes nor for any damage which might result from walkers trespassing on private property. We are anxious though that all details covering the walks are kept up to date and would therefore welcome information from readers which would be relevant to future editions.

The simple sketch maps that accompany the walks in this book are based on notes made by the author whilst checking out the routes on the ground. However, for the benefit of a proper map, we do recommend that you purchase the relevant Ordnance Survey sheet covering your walk. The Ordnance Survey maps are widely available, especially through booksellers and local newsagents.

Introduction

The next time you hear someone talk about the overcrowded south-east of England tell them to buy this book and pull on their walking boots. Bedfordshire, Buckinghamshire and Hertfordshire – just saying their names summons up images of the so-called 'shire' counties, or maybe of the Home Counties, the very heart of the south-east, but prepare to dispel any pre-conceived notions.

Their borders tucked snugly into each other like jigsaw pieces, these three counties contain a wealth of countryside, with some of the prettiest villages in the country and a number of breathtaking views. The 40 circular walks in this book present plenty of evidence of pride in, and stewardship of, that landscape as well as hope for their future preservation. Each either starts and ends near a pub or meets one halfway round, and these have been chosen to provide a variety of experience, from bistro to boozer, with all offering food.

In researching this book, Bedfordshire, known for its wide flat plains and prairie fields, has been a revelation. With the Grand Union Canal sweeping down its western edge and the River Great Ouse to the north, there's no shortage of meadows or waterside walking. Wildlife, whether fenced in, such as the deer in Woburn Park, or roaming free, is also plentiful. There's also lots of woodland and the occasional bluebell walk, as well as a myriad of thatched cottages, although the walks featured here are not shy of references to the modern world, including the former testing ground for Concorde.

The walks within the long narrow county of Buckinghamshire offer the opportunity to sample windmills, one of the country's most impressive landscaped gardens and stunning views over the Vale of Aylesbury. In addition there are a number of great houses on view such as Waddesdon Manor, West Wycombe and of course the Prime Minister's retreat of Chequers, where a public footpath sweeps past the foot of the drive. Proximity to the studios of the British film industry in the south of the county mean that many of the villages and sights covered in this book may have a certain familiarity, having featured in sets for both TV and film.

Wandering into Hertfordshire, the walker can drink in the oldest pub in the country, where Oliver Cromwell once stayed the night, or amble along wide bridleways. Clearly pioneers in the licensed trade, the county also has the country's first community-owned pub in the Red Lion in Preston, and, with Ardeley, Hertfordshire boasts perhaps one of the most beautiful village centres to be seen anywhere. Maybe we should leave it to the great wordsmith George Bernard Shaw to summarise the essence of many of the villages featured in this book. Speaking about his home and workplace, Ayot St Lawrence, Shaw said that 'the last real thing of importance that happened to it was perhaps The Flood', and often on these walks it is hard to disagree with that sentiment.

The routes featured vary between $3\frac{1}{2}$ and 7 miles. It's usually possible to leave your car in the pub cark park while you walk (but please seek the landlord's permission first), and where this isn't the case alternatives have been suggested. Each circuit has a sketch map to show

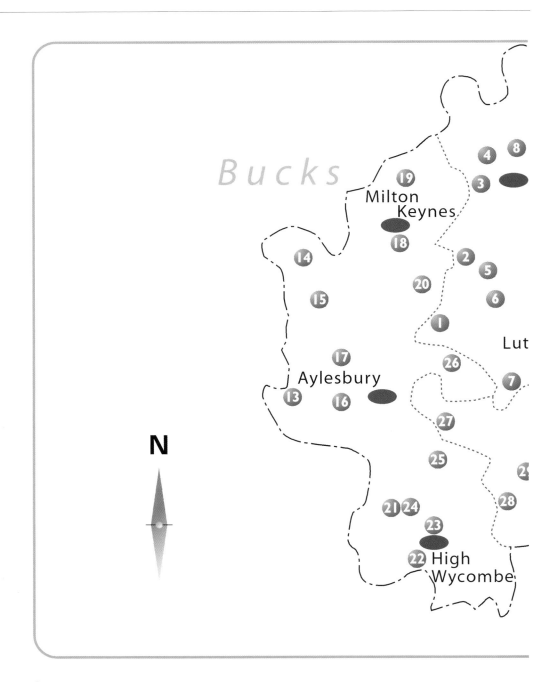

Bucks

Milton
Keynes

Aylesbury

Lut

High
Wycombe

N

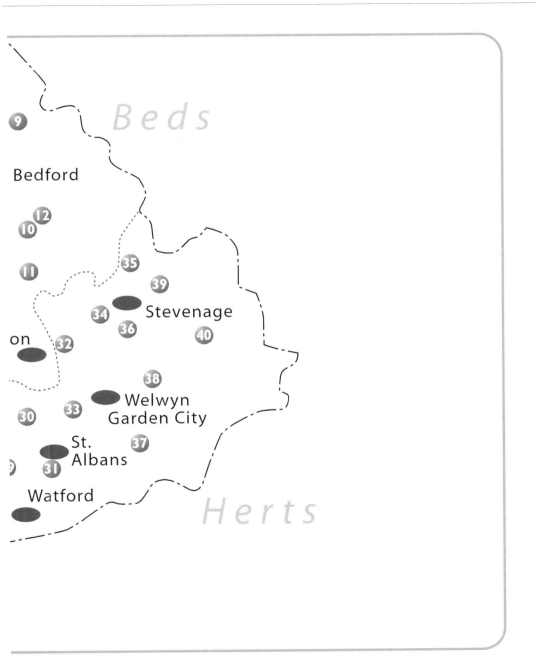

Beds

Bedford

⑨

⑫
⑩

⑪

㉟

㊴

㉞
Stevenage

㊱

⑫ on

㉜

㊵

㊳㊳

㉚

㉝

Welwyn
Garden City

St.
Albans

㊲

⑨

㉛

Watford

Herts

The River Great Ouse

you the way, but things can change and for this reason details of the relevant OS Explorer map are also provided and it is recommended that you carry one of these.

Where a walk may be particularly muddy or open to the elements this is also mentioned, but experience suggests that it's usually best to err on the side of caution and take the appropriate equipment with you. It's often possible to pause part of the way round for refreshment, but why not take a snack anyway as there's nothing better than eating al fresco with a magnificent view before you.

I have greatly enjoyed researching this book and hope that my enjoyment passes on to you as you follow in my footsteps. It would not be possible to close without thanking Sheila Roy, Matt Dudley, Les Folds, Ant Davison and Anne Fanning for their suggestions and my wife Annette for her continued support.

Happy walking!

Nick Corble

The Globe Inn

The first half of this circuit follows the route of the Greensand Ridge Walk, which is named after the rock that forms a narrow ridge across Bedfordshire and gives the area its sandy soil. Being on a ridge offers extensive views, mainly of the Ouzel valley, but these have to be earned by some steady hill climbing in the middle stages. After a steady fall across the side of the valley, the walk ends with a flat 2 mile stroll along the Grand Union Canal, starting at the photogenic Three Locks to the north of Soulbury.

The **Globe Inn** enjoys an attractive position on the very edge of the Grand Union Canal. It is reached via a precarious road over and beside the water but it is worth it. Restaurant meals and bar snacks are available, including a vegetarian Boatman's Lunch as well as burgers and bangers and mash. For others there are daily blackboard specials including a range of fish and pies. The pub is a free house serving Greene King. There is a playground for children and tables for outdoor dining.

Opening times are 11 am to 11 pm every day (12 noon to 3 pm and 6 pm to 11 pm in January and February) with food served from midday to 9 pm.

Telephone: 01525 373338.

Distance: 6 miles

OS Explorer 192 Buckingham and Milton Keynes
GR 913263

Some short steep hills and undulating in parts, but a long level stretch at the end

Starting point: The car park behind the Globe Inn. Please obtain permission to leave your car while you are walking.

How to get there: A mile north on the A4146 out of Leighton Buzzard towards Bletchley, the pub has its own road leading down to the canal.

The Walk

1 Head back to the bridge and go through the kissing gate on your right, turning immediately left on the other side to go over the raised platform that marks the beginning of the Greensand Ridge Walk. At the other end of the platform follow the signs right across the field, linking up with the river. Stay on the well-worn path over another platform and then over a bridge on the right. After the bridge keep going straight, leaving the river behind you until you meet a road. Follow this left and at the junction bear left again. You are now walking along the beginning of the ridge by the side of some woods lined with beech, pine and rhododendron. Follow the signs marked with a muntjac deer, which roam freely

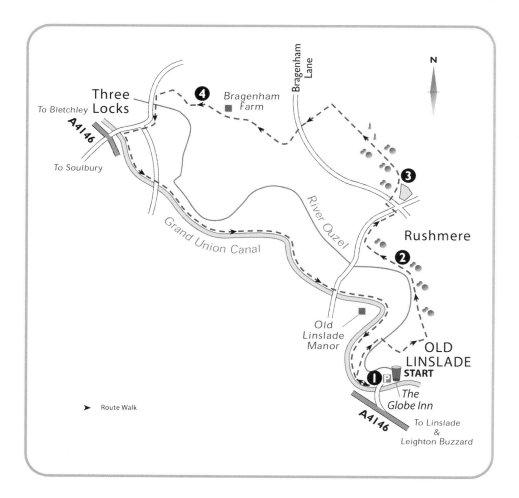

Three **Locks**
To Bletchley
A4146
To Soulbury

4 Bragenham Farm

Bragenham Lane

N

Grand Union Canal

River Ouzel

Rushmere

3

2

Old Linslade Manor

OLD LINSLADE
START
1 P
The Globe Inn
A4146
To Linslade & Leighton Buzzard

➤ Route Walk

around these parts, and where there are gaps take in the views down to your left.

❷ On exiting the woods keep to the main, uppermost, path until you reach a road. Follow the path of the road to the right, but keep within the field until it re-enters the wood. The ponds to your left on the other side of the road mark natural springs. On reaching the crossroads at Rushmere take the path 20 yards on the right down Bragenham Lane, keeping on the Greensand Ridge Walk. This curves to the left past a lake on the right. Turn left at a junction, walking uphill into the woods.

❸ Pass through the Christmas tree nursery and go over a stile. After roughly ½ mile there is a path to the left marked on a tree as the Leighton Buzzard Millennium Ramble. Take this over a stile and head half-left down back towards Bragenham Lane over an open meadow. Cross over the stile and straight over the road down an unmade track past a house. Just before a second house follow the path round to the right. This spurs to the right again and then zig-zags across some streams. Head north-west, leaving the house behind you, crossing a stile. There will be an open field to your right and a small lake on the left. Continue on this path, swinging south of Bragenham Farm, passing through some woodland.

The three locks on the Grand Union Canal at Soulbury

❹ Turn left at the stile and head downhill, keeping to the ill-defined path as much as possible as it is fairly marshy here. The path heads half-right and then straight before emerging onto a road. Turn left and downhill, past the Three Locks golf course and cross a bridge over the River Ouzel. You will come to a canal bridge, to the right of which are the picturesque three locks themselves. You turn left here, however, following the course of the canal back to the pub. This stretch has a number of long straight sections, followed by some distinct meanders, nestling in one of which is Old Linslade Manor.

Date walk completed:

....

Place of Interest

Stockgrove Country Park, just off the A5 near Great Brickhill, is run by the Greensand Trust. Highlights include ancient coppice woodland, coniferous plantations and heath, as well as a hand-dug lake and an area of oak woodland that has been designated a Site of Special Scientific Interest. Telephone: 01525 237760.

Woburn

The Black Horse

The picture book village of Woburn is an antique collector's delight, inspired no doubt by the presence of Woburn Abbey which forms a backdrop to both the village and this walk. Public footpaths enable the visitor to stroll amongst the ten different types of deer in the Deer Park as well as skirt round the formal landscaped grounds surrounding the Abbey, occasionally passing through woodland or more often walking alongside one of the many ornamental lakes. One minute you may be milling with the crowds, the next in wonderful isolation as you absorb the splendour of the grounds surrounding Duke of Bedford's Georgian home.

Distance: 6 miles

OS Explorer 192 Buckingham and Milton Keynes
GR 951332

A combination of parkland roads and gentle grassland walking, with some slight inclines; be prepared for a few boggy patches when wet

Starting point: The large (free) public car park down Park Street in the centre of Woburn.

How to get there: Woburn is 10 miles from Leighton Buzzard on the A4012 towards Bedford, 4 miles south of junction 14 on the M1.

The **Black Horse** on the main road through Woburn has a charming courtyard garden. Inside, you will find traditional wooden beams and highly polished floorboards. An open fire adds to the relaxed atmosphere on cold days. The menu offers a selection of light snacks in the bar or more formal restaurant dining. The hungry walker can chose from ploughman's and sandwiches through to whole grilled sea bass or a baked fillet of salmon stuffed with crab, washed down with a glass of wine from the wide selection on offer or maybe a pint of Greene King.

Opening times are 12 noon to 11 pm on Monday to Saturday and 12 noon to 10.30 on Sunday. Food is served from 12 noon to 2 pm and 6 pm to 9 pm on Monday to Saturday and 12 noon to 4 pm on Sunday (when busy).

Telephone: 01525 290210.

The Walk

1 Turn right out of the car park and head down towards the gate to the park. Just past the cattle grid the path bears right into the park towards a lake. Follow the path to the tip of the lake and beyond until you reach some houses and a road. Continue ahead towards the stables in front of you, passing through a gate to the left of another cattle grid. Follow the road round to the left of the stable past a rather singular house with its own ha-ha on your left. The road bends to the right alongside an elongated pond to the official entrance to the park. Let the gatekeeper know that you are sticking to the footpaths and you will be waved through.

2 Follow the road alongside another, elevated, pond until it bends to the left. At this point the footpath continues slightly to the right. There should now be views of the Abbey to your left and you are in the Deer Park, so keep an eye out! The path reaches a T-junction just before some woods, but it isn't that obvious. Take the route heading 8 o'clock to your

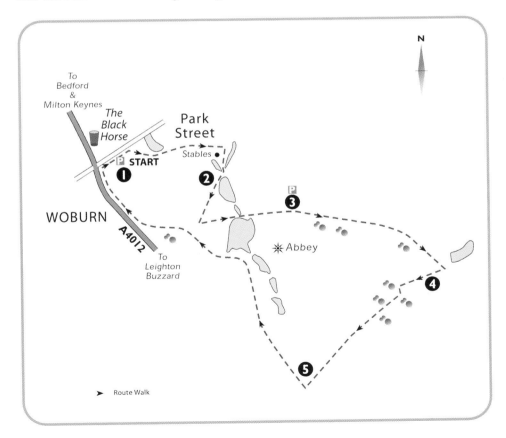

13

previous direction of travel, causing you to double back a little towards the Abbey. The path strikes out across the park but is well marked by posts. Pass through some trees and over the road to the Abbey, eventually passing off to its side to a junction of roads and the main car park.

❸ Head to the right, keeping just off the road, passing the public toilets and phone box and keeping the fence marking the perimeter of the grounds to your right. This is marked as the Greensand Ridge Walk. Head slightly uphill until the road bends to the right, at which point the path continues straight ahead towards some trees. Again, the route is well marked with posts. Go through a double gate into a small plantation, making sure to keep to the signed path. When you emerge from the trees continue downhill with a field to your left. At the end of the field cross a stream over a pair of stiles. Immediately after crossing a second stream bear right.

❹ Re-cross the stream and aim for the woods in front of you. Just before you reach these, however, a marker sends you first left and then right into the trees. The path soon bears right along a rough track following the edge of the wood, which is now on your right. When you come alongside the big brick wall, cross over a stile and over another stream. Keep the wall and ditch to your right, passing another small pond along the way. On emerging onto the edge of a field continue for 50 yards and go through a gap on the right, passing through a gate in the wall facing a half-timbered gate house.

❺ Keep by the side of the wooden fence until you reach an intersection of roads. Take the road straight ahead (marked

The splendid Woburn Abbey

with 'No Entry' signs), heading slightly uphill. The Abbey soon becomes visible again on the right. Where the road crosses a bridge over the lake take the path to the left and follow it until you reach the junction you were at earlier in the walk, this time heading left through a gate and between two fences. You are now back on the Greensand Ridge Walk. On reaching the end of the path turn right along the main road and into Woburn. Park Street and the car park are on your right and the Black Horse a few yards further on into the village.

Place of Interest

Although Woburn is synonymous with its Safari Park, **Woburn Abbey** itself is well worth a visit. It is open at weekends only from January until mid-March and from then every day from 11 am to 4 pm until the end of October. Not only are there various treasures to view but the Abbey even sells its own specially blended tea. Telephone: 01525 290666.

Date walk completed:

....

The Three Cranes

unusual cattle, with pleasant woodland paths and grassy fieldside walking, ending with a good view of the back of Turvey Abbey complete with its now derelict folly. The route passes through what was once the Abbey's grounds, although these days much of it is dedicated to the rearing of horses rather than cattle.

The **Three Cranes** next to the church has large open bars and high, beamed ceilings, with the area to the left dedicated to more formal dining and the remainder for drinking. The dining area is decorated with china curios in-cluding unusually-shaped teapots. There's also a large secluded garden. The pub specialises in unusual bar snacks, for example three bean goulash topped with gnocchi or large salads such as roasted vegetable with goat's cheese. Their steaks and sausages are also a trademark as is the traditional Turvey ploughman's.

This easy circuit is the perfect way to build up an appetite, or walk off a heavy lunch. It combines rough open grazing populated by

Opening times are 11.30 am to 3 pm and 5.30 pm to 11 pm on Monday and Tuesday; 11 am to 11 pm on Wednesday to Saturday; 12 noon to 10.30 pm on Sunday. Food is served from 12 noon to 2.30 pm and 6.30 pm to 9 pm on Monday to Saturday; 12 noon to 8 pm on Sunday.

Telephone: 01234 881305.

Distance: *4¹/₂ miles*

OS Explorer 208 Bedford and St Neots
GR 941525

Mostly field walking with the occasional slight incline

Starting point: The sweep of road off the A428 in Turvey by the pub and shops.

How to get there: Turvey lies 6 miles to the west of Bedford on the A428.

The Walk

1 Turn left out of the pub and follow the curve in the road until it meets the A428. Stay on the pavement and follow it up the left-hand side of this pretty place until just after the signs that proclaim the entrance to the village and Turvey Abbey, the 17th-century home of the Higgins family. In 1830 Charles Higgins put together his *Turvey Scrapbook* describing life in the village at that time. Pick up the footpath on the right, passing through a kissing gate, and follow the path as it strikes out half-left under a pair of horse chestnuts. On reaching a fingerpost and junction of paths bear left following a fence.

2 Pass through another kissing gate and keep your direction. On reaching a stile head out across the open space using the grain silos in the middle distance as your marker. Cross over the resulting stile and over a small plank bridge after which there's another junction of paths, where you turn right. You now pass along the side of a field with a small acreage of trees called Grotto Plantation to your right. On

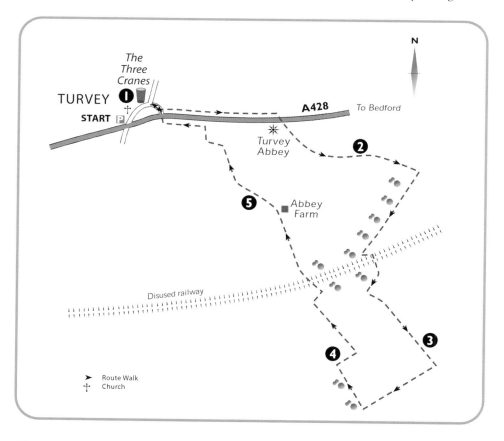

reaching the corner of the field do not go into the trees, instead drift left and then right so that they remain on your right-hand side. Keep with the edge of this, over a disused railway and then alongside a series of fields, climbing very gradually to a plateau.

❸ On reaching a Y-junction in the corner of the final field take the left-hand option and pass between two hedges. After around 50 yards there is a clearing on the right and another path, which you need to take, keeping a hedge to your right. Maintain your direction at the next junction, but at the one after that turn right, putting the trees (Hill Spinney) on your left, walking along a grassy fieldside verge. After a short while the slight fall downhill, that no doubt gave the spinney its name, commences and when the trees run out, the path curves to the right, following the right-hand boundary of a new field to the left before crossing over a small brook.

❹ There are now more trees to your left and after a short while a small pond in the corner of the field, where the path diverts to the left and this time under the disused railway. There's another small pond to the left followed by more trees and then open land, where you follow the line of the brook that feeds the pond, with the splendidly modern stables belonging to Abbey Farm in front of you. Pass through the kissing gate to your left and keep to the right of the following field until you reach yet another gate on your right.

❺ Pass through this and advance up to the driveway, where you dog-leg first left then right and down a strip of grass to a wooden fence. Pass through this and bear

Turvey Abbey

left where after 20 yards there's a metal gate on your left. Pass through this, heading half-left following a field boundary and barbed wire fence. On reaching the corner of the field turn left over the stile and continue straight ahead, keeping Turvey Abbey, the back of which now comes into view, to your right. You also pass a small turret on the edge of the Abbey's garden. On reaching a road with a cattle grid bear right and up past the back of some houses to return to the main road, where you turn left and retrace your steps back to the pub.

Place of Interest
Chicheley Hall, near Newport Pagnell and open on selected Sundays and bank holidays, was once the home of the son of Admiral Earl Beatty, a naval hero of the Great War. One of the least-altered Georgian houses in the country, the building has a Palladian hall and a hidden library. Telephone: 01234 391252.

Date walk completed:

....

17

Milton Ernest

The Queen's Head

This walk starts with a short climb to take in some excellent views over the Great Ouse Valley and out over Bedfordshire and Northants. There's also an ancient earthwork. This part of Bedfordshire is famous for its wide open fields and much of the walk involves walking either alongside or over some of these, although the route also goes through some woodland.

The **Queen's Head** is a traditional inn that also offers an à la carte menu for serious diners. The small bar contrasts with the open seating area, which is divided into two parts, one for diners and the other for drinkers. Outside there's a secluded patio. The bar menu includes delights such as seven different types of sausage, ranging from venison to wild boar and apple and taking in Mediterranean vegetables along the way. As well as the usual sandwiches and salads there's also a good selection of vegetarian dishes. Overnight accommodation is available.

Distance: 3³/₄ miles

OS Explorer 208 Bedford and St Neots GR 018561

Mainly fieldside walking, with a few steep hills

Starting point: The pub car park (with the landlord's permission).

How to get there: Milton Ernest is 8 miles north of Bedford on the A6.

Opening times Open all day for a drink, with food available from 12 noon to 2 pm and 7 pm to 9 pm.

Telephone: 01234 822412.

The Walk

1 On leaving the pub cross the road and head up Thurleigh Road opposite, going uphill as far as the church, staying on the pavement. Opposite the church take the public footpath signed to Flewton End. This starts as a stone driveway and just before the last house at the top of it you need to pass through the metal kissing gate on the right. Cut half-left across the resulting open space to a stile, which is about 20 yards higher than the more prominent gate further down. After this, cross immediately over another stile to the right and proceed forward along the side of a large ditch.

2 This ditch is in fact an historical earthwork of uncertain origin and the path climbs steadily along its edge. When the earthwork runs out pause to take in the view behind you, which incorporates the Great Ouse Valley. Ahead is a water tower belonging to an industrial park. Maintain your direction, keeping the field

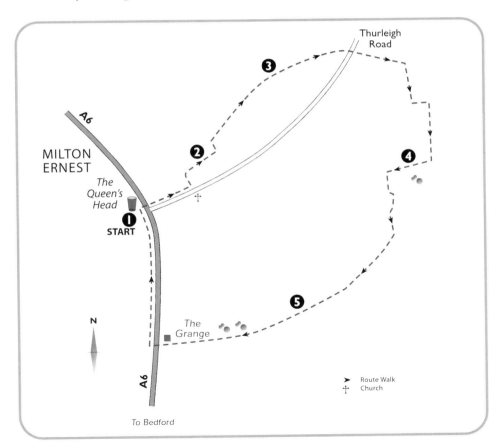

Thurleigh
Road

3

A6

MILTON
ERNEST

The
Queen's
Head

2

4

†

1

START

N

The
Grange

5

➤ Route Walk
† Church

A6

To Bedford

19

boundary to your left, and at the top of the hill there's another excellent view, this time incorporating the river itself. It can get quite windy up here, but both the view and the teeming wildlife that inhabit the traditional hedgerows make it worthwhile. It's also worth looking up to see if you can spot birds of prey.

❸ On coming to a curve in the field continue in the same direction, cutting across the middle of the field and heading for some trees. When you reach the woods turn right along their edge until you come to the road, where you need to cross over and pick up the path once again. The path now follows along the perimeter fence of an industrial complex, which at this point seems very quiet but is clearly important to someone given the security involved. You need to follow the fence until it comes to a corner where you turn left onto a very minor road. After about 20 yards turn right and pick up the fence again, heading for some more trees.

❹ Once again, follow the fence round the edge of the wood. After a couple of turns you finally lose your metal companion, picking up instead a hedge. Follow this as it zig-zags along and on reaching the end of the field turn right through a clearing onto a dirt track. This is a public bridleway and it passes between two fields, becoming steadily firmer, in time passing along the left-hand side of some more woods. Once again, it is very open here and it can get quite windy.

❺ When the metalled road finally decides to curve you need to continue straight ahead on a path delineated by two wooden fences. This leads out onto a road, which you cross, picking up the

One of the magnificent vistas seen around Milton Ernest

path on the other side. There is a very steep descent into trees here but you immediately turn left into a field, keeping the woods to your right as you descend down a slope. Pass through a gap on the right and follow the path downhill for a few hundred yards, turning first left then right and ending by The Grange, a private house with its own ponds. Pass through the gate ahead of you and follow the drive to the right bringing you back up onto the A6. Here you need to cross the road and use the pavement to head right back into Milton Ernest.

Place of Interest

Bromham Mill and Gallery, on the A428 west of Bedford, sits on the Great Ouse where it is spanned by a 26-arch bridge. The mill has a huge iron waterwheel but today is used mainly as an art gallery, which also offers tea. Open afternoons on Wednesday to Saturday and all day on Sunday and bank holidays from March to October. Telephone: 01234 824330.

Date walk completed:

....

An undemanding circuit with some hills which means that, unusually for Bedfordshire, this walk offers not one but two magnificent vistas over the surrounding countryside. The route skirts the edge of the grounds of Woburn Abbey, and halfway through progresses down a mile-long avenue of trees. A scattered village, Milton Bryan is notorious for being the location of a specially-built transmitter station used to broadcast 'black propaganda' to Nazi Germany during the Second World War. A link to the Great War also exists with Battlesden House, whose converted outhouses were used as a holiday home for weary nurses during that conflict.

Distance: *4½ miles*

OS Explorer 192 Buckingham and Milton Keynes
GR 974302

Even walking with some not too challenging hills; some mud at the beginning in winter

Starting point: The Red Lion car park (with the owner's permission).

How to get there: Milton Bryan is less than a mile off the A4012 just south of Woburn. The pub lies to the south of the village.

The **Red Lion** is a tastefully modernised village pub at the south end of Milton Bryan near to the duck pond, which is hidden away behind a hedge. There's a large car park with a garden but the pub is really all about its restaurant, which takes up the majority of the interior. That said, the public bar manages to retain much of its old charm. Be prepared to indulge in fresh local produce such as dry cured ham and organic fried eggs or seared escalope of salmon. The bar serves a good selection of wines as well as freshly squeezed orange and apple juice.

Opening times are 11 am to 3 pm and 6.30 pm to 11 pm on Monday to Saturday; 12 noon to 3 pm on Sunday. Food is served from 12 noon to 2.30 pm and 7.30 pm to 9.30 pm Monday to Saturday. No food is available on Sunday.

Telephone: 01525 210044.

The Walk

1 Head off down the No Through Road opposite the pub, passing a pond on your left, until you reach a kink in the road. Take the footpath in the corner, which lies by another pond hidden behind trees on your right. This immediately curves to the right to a junction of paths and you need to take the right-hand option, which cuts across a field towards a yellow-tipped marker pole. Pass through the hedge and across the following field until you reach the busy A4012.

2 Cross the stile and then the road and head up the lane signposted to Battlesden, taking in the spectacular view over to Dunstable and its famous downs on your left. The road offers easy walking after the field and crests a hill before falling down again between hedges into Battlesden itself. On reaching the bottom of the hill stick with the road, doubling back on yourself before heading uphill again towards a telephone mast on your left. There are more good views here looking out over Battlesden Park towards Stockgrove Country Park. The road now

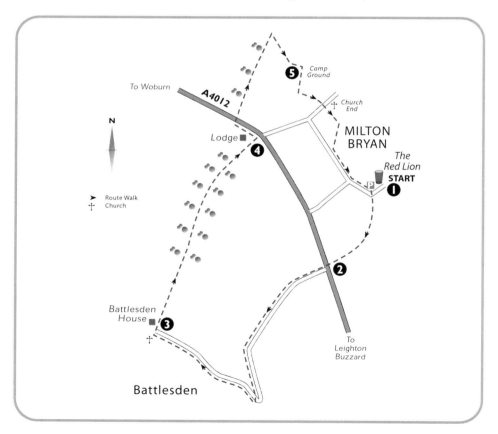

heads steeply down into a dip before rising again, aiming all the time for the somewhat lonely-looking church on the top of the hill in front of you. This is the church of St Peter, which is distinguished by having no aisle. Parts of the building are 13th century, with various later additions.

3 On reaching the top of the hill the footpath is quite determinedly signposted to the right of the green gates leading to Battlesden House, a magnificent private residence guarded by a majestic willow. It is easy to imagine how the tired nurses stationed here during the Great War would have found peace and a chance to relax. Continue up the track on the other side of the house and stay with it along Battlesden Avenue – a mile of trees, some of which appear quite gnarled and the stuff of childish nightmares, whilst others have fallen victim to the gales blowing in from the open fields. One of the entrances to nearby Woburn Abbey becomes clearly visible to the left towards the end of the avenue.

4 By way of contrast to the ragged state of the trees, the avenue ends rather more grandly with a lodge house and gated entrance back on the A4012. Cross over the road again and walk along the verge downhill to the left, heading towards the entrance to Woburn seen a few minutes earlier. Before reaching this, however, a stile on the right takes you into a field, where you follow along the edge of some trees and a brick wall marking the limit of the Abbey's grounds. Ignore the path to your left taking you to a rather attractive half-timbered house and keep instead to the top of the field, where you turn right, keeping with the field on the outside of the

The duck pond at Milton Bryan

fence and aiming for another yellow-tipped pole.

5 Continue through the Scouts' camping ground and turn right where indicated through another (much less grand) avenue of trees, following the concrete path as it twists left, right and then left again. This eventually emerges by St Peter's church, appropriately enough at Church End. Continue down the shingle driveway past Manor Farmhouse and then through some trees to a wooden gate where you cross half-right over some open ground and then across a stile onto a local road. Turn left here and walk along the pathway back to the pub.

Place of Interest
Woburn Heritage Centre is housed in the remains of the old parish church and includes a small museum detailing the history of the village and the Abbey. Telephone: 01525 290631.

Date walk completed:

23

Toddington

The Sow and Pigs

Starting by the motte of a long-ago abandoned castle, this walk sweeps round through a geological gap exploited in modern times by both the motorway and railway, allowing the walker excellent views from either side. There's also the opportunity to witness the outputs of a bio-diversity project where woodland is being managed using ancient coppicing techniques and wildflower species are being allowed to recover. Parts of the walk are challenging, but there's a pub halfway round if you feel the need to recharge the batteries.

The **Sow and Pigs**, a Greene King pub in Church Square near the centre of Toddington, is one of those places you thought had disappeared but clings tenaciously to tradition. The large tables require you to socialise with your neighbours and one even has a cribbage board inlaid into its top. There's an open fireplace and a games corner and even an old piano that begs to be played.

Distance: *6 miles*

OS Explorer 193 Luton and Stevenage GR 011289

Mainly fieldside walking with one or two steady hills

Starting point: Conger Lane behind the church near the library.

How to get there: Toddington lies on the A5120 between Flitwick and Dunstable.

The pub offers an all day breakfast and a comprehensive menu of freshly prepared dishes including salmon fish cakes, Chinese chilli pork and noodles and spicy meat and cheese platters.

Opening times are 11 am to 11 pm on Monday to Saturday; 12 noon to 10.30 pm on Sunday. Food is served from 11 am to 4 pm every day.

Telephone: 01525 873089.

The Walk

1 Pick up the signpost for the Icknield Way by a thatched house on the left-hand side of Conger Lane. Go over the stile and head towards the mound on the right. This striking feature is the motte of an old castle. Cross a pair of stiles either side of a horse pasture and pick up the path to the top of the cemetery, turning left at the corner. On reaching the gate bear right, pausing briefly to enjoy the views over the valley below on your left. The path soon heads downhill left over a pair of small wooden bridges and some stiles. This stretch can get thick with nettles in season so some kind of protection is advisable. Continue over the next stile down the left-hand side of a field.

2 On reaching the road cross over and continue in a north-easterly direction with Mill Farm on your left. Cross over another bridge and bear left. Continue following the edge of the field until you meet a road where you turn right and cross over the motorway. Bear left at the junction the other side of the bridge and pick up the footpath on the right just before the farmhouse. Pass to the right of the barns and follow the yellow route posts heading east, keeping with the track at the junction of paths. You should now be walking parallel with the motorway.

3 At a bend in the track the path cuts across some open ground to the left of a pylon. Maintain your direction and pass the second pylon to the right. Pass under

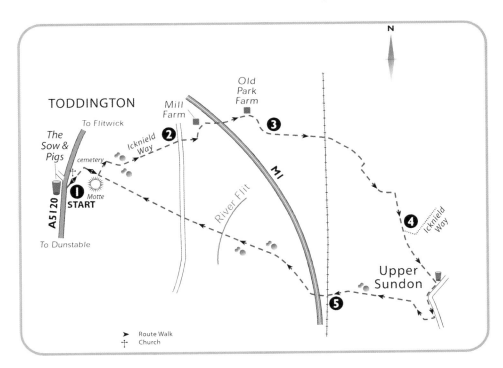

the railway and pick up the path on the other side, still heading east between two hedges. On reaching a field turn right and follow the boundary round to the right. Continue along the edge of the next field, ignoring the alternative to the left. The path curves round to the left and after a hundred yards turns right to follow the side of a copse along a well-worn surface.

4 On reaching a wooden gate you bid the Icknield Way farewell and head half-right across the field to its top right-hand corner where you pick up an unmade road that leads you into Upper Sundon. Emerging next to the Red Lion (01525 875806) turn right and follow the road round until you reach a sign for the Chiltern Way opposite a bus stop. Take this across the corner of a field and turn right down the road on the other side. Before heading down the road you may wish to take in the view where the path continues the other side of the hedge. The road heads steadily downhill, curving down until it meets a tall hedge where the route again becomes a footpath heading west.

5 A pair of bridges allow you to re-cross both the motorway and railway respectively. Take the path immediately on the right after the second of these. This starts out parallel to the motorway before cutting across a field with an electricity plant on your distant left. Continue along the left-hand side of a new hedge to Hipsey Spinney, an area of woodland that is being maintained as part of the Bedfordshire bio-diversity project using traditional coppicing, which is much in evidence. This and the next set of woods, which you pass to the right, have useful information signs. Cross the River Flit

The River Flit

and on reaching a road cross over. Maintain a north-westerly direction across fields as the path becomes more of a track aiming for the right on the church spire ahead. Soon you return to the motte and from here simply retrace your steps to where you started.

Place of Interest
Sundon Hills Country Park, just north of Upper Sundon, is a mix of beech and ash woodland perched on one of the highest points in Bedfordshire. It is also a Site of Special Scientific Interest with part of the John Bunyan Trail passing through it. There's room to park and picnic and spectacular views. Telephone: 01582 608489.

Date walk completed:

....

The Bell

walk the route cuts across a local golf course and then edges along the boundary of Whipsnade Wildlife Park, and on most days it is possible to see herds of the deer that have made the park famous.

The Bell is a cosy restaurant and pub on the edge of the village exuding an air of being both part of the local community as well as a haunt of visitors. Low oak beams and horsebrasses set the tone for a menu of traditional pub fare, as well as a decent selection of more adventurous blackboard specials such as shoulder of lamb in red berries. The pub specialises in home-made pies and sausages and has a very tempting dessert menu. Beers include Fuller's London Pride and Morland Old Speckled Hen and there is an extensive wine list. The pub welcomes children and has a good beer garden outside.

Opening times are 11.30 am to 3 pm and 6 pm to 11 pm on Monday to Saturday; 12 noon to 3 pm and 7 pm to 10.30 pm on Sunday. Food is served 12 noon to 2.30 pm and 7 pm to 9.30 pm Monday to Saturday and all day on Sunday.

Telephone: 01582 872460.

S tarting in the attractive hidden-away village of Studham, this walk cuts across the broad expanse of Studham Common and goes on to explore the local beech woodlands dotted around the vicinity. Large open fields in between give an opportunity to admire both the fertility of the local soil as well as expansive views. In the middle of the

Distance: *6¹/₄ miles*

OS Explorer 182 St Albans and Hatfield GR 123160

The walk is mainly through fields and woodland with some gentle hills

Starting point: The Bell's car park. Please obtain permission to leave your car while you walk.

How to get there: Studham is north of the A4146 between Hemel Hempstead and Leighton Buzzard and just south-east of Whipsnade.

The Walk

1 From the pub head back downhill to the memorial clock on the edge of the common. Pick up the footpath running along the right-hand edge of the football pitch and into some trees, ignoring the second path that heads uphill into the woods proper. You should now be walking parallel to the road. Go to the left of The Old School and stick to the right of the field boundary, the new school being on your right. Cross the road and continue straight ahead, again ignoring the offer to head up into the woods on the left and other possible diversions, crossing a number of stiles as you go.

2 Eventually, the path bears right into a wood – Mason's Plantation, a magnificent collection of beech trees. Follow the edge of this and at the T-junction turn right and continue round to the left after a hundred yards. Keep straight on at the next junction until you emerge into open fields on your right. Cut the corner off the next field and follow the path through a gap in the hedge on the right where you

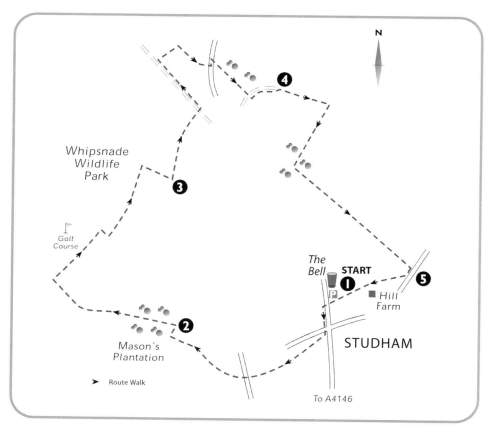

will find yourself on a golf course. Keep going straight ahead, but take the partial protection of the avenue of immature trees. Halfway down this the path diverts to the right (it is clearly signed) and you now cut across a number of fairways, so keep your eyes peeled for loose golf balls. You are now on part of the Icknield Way. The path dog-legs slightly to the right but keep your direction until you reach the edge of the course. Your route continues along the field that abuts the Whipsnade Wildlife Park, where you can usually see herds of deer.

Herds of deer in Whipsnade Park can often be seen from the path

❸ Follow the left-hand edge of this field, going right, left and then right again and at the T-junction turn left along a high hedge and straight on through woods. At the corner with the Wildlife Park turn left down a partially-metalled road. Where this meets another road coming from the left take the path to the right through a kissing gate into a field. After the second kissing gate turn right. Cross the road and pick up the footpath heading right with woods on the left. On reaching the housing follow the road round as it curves left and take the footpath downhill on the right by number 25.

❹ On reaching the road turn right but keep to the top of the bank and at the end of the housing bear right again. Keep to the edge, ignoring the offers to head back into the houses. Follow this along for a while where it briefly opens up and shortly after re-entering some woods take the path to the right through the woods for a short while. On leaving the trees there is a long straight path across a field, with your destination marked by some houses. The path goes to the right of a small woodland grove and then goes down an alleyway along the side of the houses.

❺ On reaching a road turn right and just after Hill Farm pick up the footpath again and head for the bottom left-hand corner of the next two fields, crossing three stiles along the way. Head for the top right-hand corner of the next large field and cross straight over, going over some stiles through the top of some horse pastures. Keep the woods to your right and you will emerge onto an alleyway that brings you out to the side of the Bell.

Place of Interest

The Whipsnade Tree Cathedral, 2 miles south of Dunstable, was planted during the First World War in a spirit of faith, hope and reconciliation, and was laid out in the shape of a medieval cathedral. Entrance is free and a service is held there every year on 15th June. Telephone: 01582 872406.

Date walk completed:

....

Thurleigh
The Jackal

the traditional bedrock of the local economy. By way of contrast the walk also offers the chance to stroll alongside a more modern generator of wealth, the Bedford Technology Park. Once an airfield capable of accepting Concorde, this is now a hive of more up to date activity.

The **Jackal** has two tastefully decorated bars and each has a mix of traditional chairs and sofas, while photos featuring regulars at various pub events emphasise that this is a 'local' as well as a restaurant. The proprietors are justly proud of their food and the menu includes a good range of soups as well as traditional dishes, with a dash of the Asian-Pacific giving extra zing such as chicken breast served with Thai green curry sauce and rice or whole sea bass with deep fried fennel citrus sauce. Sweets are a particular signature, ranging from sticky toffee pudding to Belgian chocolate towers.

With a converted windmill at its centre, this route manages to include not only the chance to sample a small Bedfordshire village but also the vast prairies that have stood as

Distance: *4¹/₂ miles*

OS Explorer 208 Bedford and St Neots GR 052587

A few bumpy footpaths mean that good footwear is required, but otherwise some gentle hills and footpath walking

Starting point: The pub car park (with the landlord's permission) or from the side road.

How to get there: Thurleigh lies 2 miles north-east of Milton Ernest on the A6 north of Bedford.

Opening times are 12 noon to 3 pm and 6 pm to 11 pm on Tuesday to Sunday (10.30 pm on Sunday). Food is served from 12 noon to 2 pm and 7 pm to 9 pm on Tuesday to Saturday; 12 noon to 2 pm on Sunday.

Telephone: 01234 771293.

The Walk

1 Turn left out of the pub and head left up through the village, walking uphill using the pathway provided. Pass the village hall and the road to Keysoe and pick up the footpath on the right just after Chapelfields. This takes you through private property initially via a green metal gate, a wooden one and then a stile, after which you turn left along the edge of some land. After about 50 yards, beyond the metal storage building, turn right where the path follows the right-hand edge of a field sloping gently downhill and then bear right at a corner in the field. The path now heads half-left across a field where, on the other side, there's a small gap in a hedge, which you need to pass through.

2 You should now get your first glimpse of the converted windmill, with its glass casement at the top, on the edge of Thurleigh over towards your right. Maintain your direction and cross over a small brook. Continue through a gap in the hedge to an open field where you cross over, aiming for a small cottage with intricate thatching on the horizon. This brings you out onto a road (Mill Road) where you need to turn right and head straight down towards the windmill. On reaching the T-junction on which the

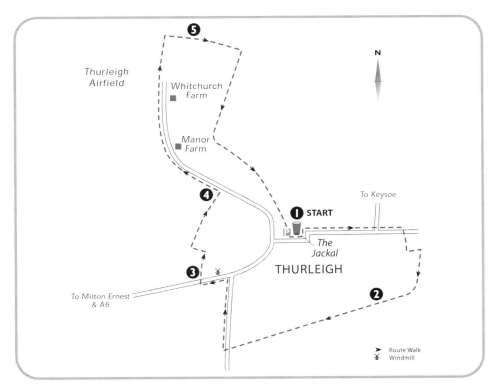

windmill stands turn left into Milton Road and pick up the footpath on your immediate right.

3 You should now spot Thurleigh Airfield. In the 1960s, prototype Concordes were landed here, but these days it's used as a technology and business park. Follow the right-hand edge of the field down to the bottom corner where you pick up a small wooden bridge over a brook, although you may need to take care here as it can become overgrown. Having crossed the bridge turn left and then right at the hedge in front of you. Maintain the hedge to your left as it dissolves into a classic English hedgerow with blackberries, sloes and rose hips coming together to make a colourful sight in summer.

4 The path eventually emerges onto a road via a stile where you need to turn left, heading towards the airfield. Follow the road round to the right as it passes Manor Farm and just after an MOD sign pick up the footpath to your left next to the airfield perimeter fence, avoiding the private road to Whitwick Farm. Continue past the farm, sticking with the fence as it swings round to the right. The going can get quite rough here and sturdy footwear is recommended. On coming to a corner in the fence, where it makes a sharp left turn by the old air traffic control tower, emerge onto an open field and pick up the path that heads right, following the line of the airfield perimeter but in the opposite direction, keeping Whitwick Farm to your right.

5 Aim for the line of trees in front of you. You are now walking across one of the vast Bedfordshire grain prairies where

An attractive thatched cottage in Thurleigh

the flat landscape is dominated by cultivated fields. On reaching a yellow-tipped marker post pick up the path to your right. On reaching a corner in the field head left and pick up your direction again, this time keeping Manor Farm to your right. The windmill again comes into view over in the middle distance to the left. On reaching some trees strike out half-left using the church spire as a landmark. This brings you out along a hedge and eventually down alongside a brook, where you meet up with another path and emerge onto the road just by the pub.

Place of Interest
Bedford Butterfly Park in Wilden, south-east of Thurleigh, has a Tropical Butterfly House and Insect Room and a farm, as well as a teashop. The park celebrates the diversity of the English countryside and is open daily from February to October. Telephone: 01234 772770.

Date walk completed:
....

Keysoe lies at the northern end of the Bedfordshire grain belt. This walk offers a wonderful opportunity to wander amongst the large open fields so characteristic of this area and to enjoy expansive views over the remainder of the county and beyond. There is a delightful arbour about halfway round, which provides welcome shade on a hot day. The views require some climbing so good footwear is recommended, but the result is worth the effort.

The **Chequers** has had the same landlords for a quarter of a century so you'd expect them to have hit on the right formula for a traditional country pub and they've certainly succeeded. Two bars are separated by a large open fireplace. Some very low beams act as a challenge for taller patrons. There's a large function room at the back as well as a patio and garden. Food ranges from roasted peppers to lamb shank with rosemary gravy, and the chef also does a mean steak.

Opening times are 11.30 am (12 noon on Sunday) to 2.30 pm and 6.30 pm to 11 pm (8.30 on Sunday). Food is served from 12 noon to 2 pm and 7 pm to 9.30 pm. The pub is shut on Tuesdays.

Telephone: 01234 607678.

Distance: *4 miles*

OS Explorer 225 Huntingdon and St Ives GR 076633

A steep climb at the beginning but otherwise mainly fieldside walking

Starting point: The car park at the Chequers (with the landlord's permission).

How to get there: Keysoe lies on the B660 about 6 miles north of Bedford.

33

The Walk

1 Turn right out of the pub and then right again down Riseley Road. Go past the telephone box and tar-painted farm buildings and pick up the footpath on the right on a bend in the road next to a thatched cottage. Follow this downhill past another thatched cottage and alongside a rather prickly hedgerow to a dirt track where you turn left. About halfway along the resulting field a marker sends you to the left where you follow the new field boundary along until you come to a gap in the hedge with a plank bridge

over a small brook. Do not pass through this, but rather pick up the path on your right just before the gap.

2 You should now have a hedge to your left and a large open field to the right. Depending on the season this may be a blanket of green or a cloth of gold. The path now heads steadily uphill, kinking slightly to the right as you near the top. On reaching the first kink pause both to take breath and to admire the views over towards the north-east over Cambridgeshire. Keep with the field boundary as it curves further to the right

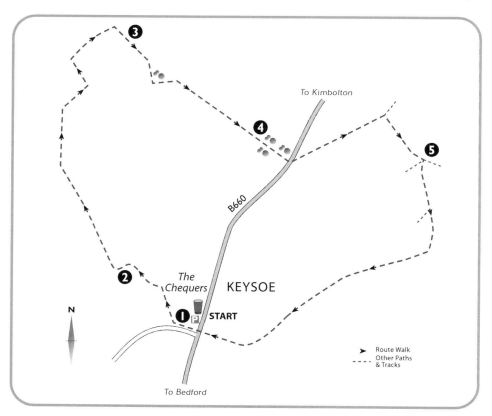

and when it reaches a corner cut into the next field bear left, with the path heading steadily uphill again after a short respite on the flat. At the end of this field follow the sign directing you to the right and along a clearly distinguishable track heading downhill towards some trees.

3 The track soon gains a more solid surface and after a few hundred yards there's a choice of paths to the right. You need to take the one sending you to the right-hand edge of a spinney, that is sharp right rather than half-left. Continue towards the trees and on reaching them take the gap in the hedge on your right which allows you to skirt round them, keeping the trees to your left until you reach the corner of the spinney. Here there's another convenient gap in the hedge and you now need to head right, downhill, through the centre of a large field, ignoring the path to your left along the edge of the trees.

4 Towards the end of the field at the bottom of the hill the path enters a delightful channel between and underneath trees and comes out on the other side next to a large house complete with swimming pool, and from there onto the road. Turn right here and then almost immediately left, picking up the marked footpath, which sends you sharp left. Continue with this acute direction using a permissive path cutting half-right across the field (this may not always be clear, but it does exist and is marked) until you reach an opening in the hedge ahead. Now bear right, keeping the hedge to your left and avoiding moving into the next field.

5 On reaching a junction of paths at the

One of the wide views near Keysoe

next hedge turn right again, keeping both the hedge and the ditch to your left and ignoring the plank bridge which takes you through the hedge. On reaching a new ditch turn left and pick up the path, bearing slightly right and using the church spire in the middle distance as a marker. You will come to a yellow-tipped pole where you need to pass over the stile and maintain your direction. Go over another stile and after a short while turn right through a large gap and proceed down the side of a small piece of grazing where another stile brings you out, rather conveniently, in front of the pub.

Place of Interest
Grafham Water in Cambridgeshire, 5 miles north-east of Keysoe, is set in 1,500 acres of countryside and has a large nature reserve with information boards, a special dragonfly pond and a wildlife garden, as well as a café attached to a visitor centre. Telephone: 01480 812154.

Date walk completed:

....

The Black Horse

This is not the Ireland of shamrocks and leprechauns but rather a pretty collection of houses a few miles outside Bedford surrounded by pine forests. This easy circuit sandwiches an amble through the trees and stretches of roadside walking with a number of unusual sights along the way, including a nursery of semi-mature trees, a folly and an unusual style of thatching. As well as the Black Horse there are two further pubs, allowing walkers to stretch this route out to take the best part of a day should they so wish.

The **Black Horse** on the edge of this small hamlet is a popular stopping off point for after-work drinkers and those looking for a quiet rural location for a meal. The pub is deservedly well known both for its beer (Greene King) and its food, with separate lunch and dinner menus. For lunch you may be tempted by smoked duck with watercress and Asian pear salad or wild mushroom and chive risotto, whilst evening diners can enjoy dishes such as slow-baked lemon-peppered lamb shank or ballottine of corn-fed chicken. The chef also caters well for vegetarians.

Opening times are 11.30 am to 3 pm and 6 pm to 11 pm on Monday to Saturday; 12 noon to 6 pm on Sunday. Food is served 12 noon to 2.30 pm Monday to Saturday and 12 noon to 4.30 pm on Sunday.

Telephone: 01462 811398.

Distance: *5¹/₂ miles*

OS Explorer 208 Bedford and St Neots GR 134414

Mostly rural roadside walking with a stretch through pleasant woodland in the middle

Starting point: The Black Horse.

How to get there: Ireland lies just to the north of the B658 near its junction with the A600 linking Shefford with Bedford.

The Walk

1 Turn left out of the pub car park and follow the road round to a fork in the road where you head right and downhill amongst some woodland and under a disused railway bridge. At the end of this road there's a T-junction with some tan coloured cottages in front of you where you need to turn right, passing under another railway bridge, and swinging left round the bend. Continue on the road for a couple of hundred yards until you meet a track on the right leading down to a sawmill, also marked as a public footpath.

Go down this over an open area, passing to the left of the tar-covered wooden barn where the road bends to the right, passing by an elegant-looking house on your left. The track becomes slightly less firm here but still represents very easy walking.

2 Shortly after the house the path swings to the left, utilising a wooden bridge over a small stream and continues in a northerly direction, with trees to the left and a field to your right. Pass a cottage and continue straight ahead until you reach Warden Lodge and another junction of roads. Here you need to follow the road straight ahead signposted to Ickwell, keeping the pretty thatched Old Warden Lodge to your right. The road runs slightly uphill for a while along a lane that is in fact distinguished by a series of attractive thatched cottages, a feature of which is the way the thatch is fashioned in curves around the windows. Also look out for the old School House with its unusual roof line as well as red builders' marks high up on some of the houses, most of which date back to the late 19th century.

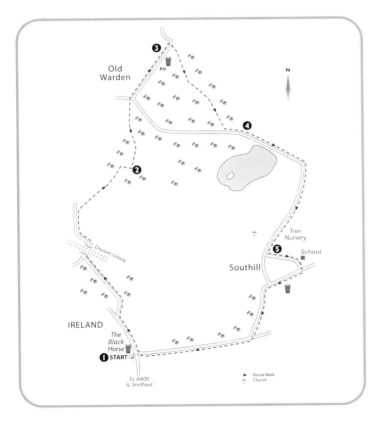

3 Pass over the brow of the hill and down the other side past the post office and Hare and Hounds Inn (Tel. 01727 627225, Charles Wells beers), both of which are on your right. Opposite the old village pump, hidden away in its own brick and tile enclosure, and just before the curve in the road, the footpath heads uphill on the right into the trees. This is initially quite a steep climb, but not for long and soon results in a long gentle stroll downhill amongst tall pines, all of which are probably destined for the sawmill you passed earlier. Stick to the clearly defined path through the trees until you eventually meet a kissing gate and a road where you turn left.

4 Walk along the road where soon there are glimpses of a lake, complete with its own folly, on the right, but sadly this is on private land and you will have to satisfy yourself with only a glimpse. Stick with the road as it curves round to the right and then enters a long straight which eventually brings you into Southill, with the tower of that village's All Saints' church visible amongst the tree tops over to the right.

5 Pass the tree and shrub nursery, where all manner of trees can be seen at different stages of maturity sitting in rows in their pots, and turn left at the junction that follows into School Lane. Turn right at the next T-junction next to the children's play area and opposite a cottage sporting a 1796 marker and continue past the White Horse pub (01462 813364, Greene King and Fuller's beers) that soon comes up on your left. On reaching yet another

The well at Old Warden

T-junction turn right and follow the long straight road until you reach a grass triangle where you turn right and find yourself back at the pub.

Place of Interest

The Shuttleworth Collection of historic vehicles and aeroplanes just outside Old Warden (01767 627288) offers spectacular displays ranging from the very first flying machines through to Spitfires and beyond. The first Sunday of every month is a 'flying day' when you can see the machines in action. Telephone: 01767 627288.

Date walk completed:

....

The Musgrave Arms

This varied walk has at its centrepiece a tantalising glimpse of Wrest Park. Now part of an agricultural research institute, the house was originally the home of the de Grey family who are perhaps best remembered for their tea. The impressive gardens are tended by English Heritage and are open to the public on weekends during the summer. The house is approached via fields and appears suddenly at the brow of a hill, whilst the route afterwards goes through woods. Much of the walking is along country roads, making it easy to cover the distance.

The **Musgrave Arms** prides itself on its range of beers, many of which are served from barrels inset into the wall behind the bar so that they are gravity-fed. Inside there are several separate areas where you can eat or simply enjoy a game of cribbage – in front of a welcoming fire in winter. There's a large outdoor area and car park at the rear of the pub and an efficient kitchen offering bar snacks such as bacon and mushroom baguettes through to more formal dining such as pan fried lemon sole or calves' liver and bacon. There's also a tempting selection of sweets including rum and raisin ice cream and the unusual sounding Bailey's cheesecake.

Opening times are 12 noon to 3 pm and 5 pm to 11 pm on Monday to Friday; 12 noon to 11 pm on Saturday; 12 noon to 4 pm and 7 pm to 11 pm on Sunday. Food is served from 12 noon to 2 pm and 7 pm to 9 pm (8.30 pm on Sunday).

Telephone: 01462 711286.

Distance: $6^3/_4$ *miles*

OS Explorer 193 Luton and Stevenage GR 122328

Mostly even roads and paths with two reasonably demanding gradients

Starting point: The car park of the Musgrave Arms in Apsley End just south of Shillington (with the landlord's permission).

How to get there: Apsley End is a mile north of the B655 linking Hitchin and Barton-le-Clay north of Luton.

39

The Walk

1 Turn left out of the pub car park and along the pavement, following the stream up to a junction where you turn right and then immediately left up High Road, maintaining a northerly direction. On reaching Shillington proper turn left up Church Street, just after the petrol garage and post office. This heads uphill and you need to keep to the road on the left where it forks until you reach the church itself. Turn right into the churchyard, passing in front of the entrance until you reach open ground occupied by allotments with a good view to the left. The path now heads steadily downhill and on reaching a junction bear left and downhill some more to another junction where you turn right into Bury Road.

2 After a couple of hundred yards

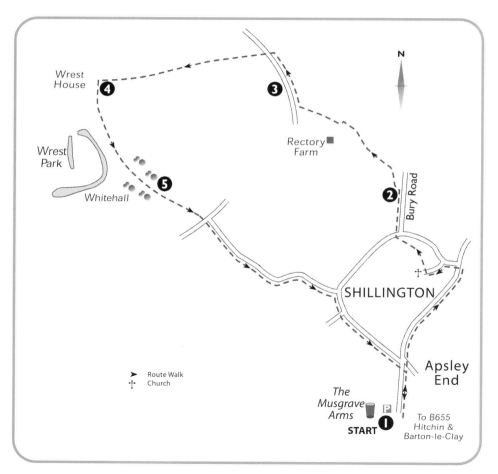

there's a gap in the houses and a crossroads of footpaths. Take the left-hand fork over the stream heading down a track but turn immediately right over a stile to follow the stream round the back of some houses. Follow the path to a bridge, which you cross and then cut across a field, the main path of the stream now flowing on your left. Cross over some more water and turn left then right to follow the left-hand edge of a field past Rectory Farm all the way to a road where you turn right.

❸ Quite a steep climb follows, but it's not too bad and is on an even surface. Continue to a point just before the end of the houses, where you cross the road and join a bridleway on the left. Initially a dirt track this soon becomes a concrete road and is again steadily uphill but relatively undemanding. The reward for your effort follows when you crest the top of the hill and a vista of Wrest Park and its grounds spreads out before you. The path is now downhill, bringing you towards the house. The fields here are used to grow experimental crops and it's worth keeping an eye open for the unusual!

❹ The route takes you along the side of the buildings to the left, but it is worthwhile wandering up the road first to get a glimpse of the house itself, which looks as if it would be more at home in Central Europe than the heart of Bedfordshire, its style being heavily influenced by Versailles Palace amongst other chateaux. Return to the path and glimpse over into the gardens on the right with their collection of different species of trees as well as statuary and pavilions. It's also just possible to see the lake. The trees on your left are particularly well endowed

Wrest Park

with mistletoe and are therefore highly popular with the locals at Christmas.

❺ The path now enters woods and passes an impressive house part-hidden behind trees with the imposing name of Whitehall. The woods also include a number of horse jumps, some of which seem to have been adopted by local children. On reaching the road continue straight ahead, following it as it turns first left then right, arriving at another T-junction where you turn right, signposted to Pirton. Follow this back to the junction at Apsley End encountered at the beginning of the walk and turn right back to the pub.

Place of Interest

Wrest Park, just east of Silsoe, boasts one of the best formal gardens in England. Opening is restricted to summer weekends and bank holidays but once inside there's a wealth of places to explore and wander in. Telephone: 01525 860152.

Date walk completed:

....

The White Horse

A short, flat walk giving the opportunity to wander alongside the delightful River Ivel and pop in on the last surviving independent flour mill in Bedfordshire. The walk starts from an archetypal village green and wanders across fields, including a wildflower meadow, before reaching the river. The route continues by winding its way alongside the water before reaching an ancient bridge and the mill, after which there's a short stretch of road bringing you back to your starting point.

Distance: *3¹/₂ miles*

OS Explorer 208 Bedford and St Neots
GR 172427

Largely even paths with some field and riverside walking

Starting point: The village green in Broom.

How to get there: Broom lies just off the B658 a mile south-west of Biggleswade.

The **White Horse** on the village green in Broom is a 17th-century Grade II listed building spread over several levels and has an oak-beamed fireplace. The pub is a family run business stretching back over three generations and it shows. There's a warm welcome and good food, especially Sunday lunches, with this meal being the highlight of the week and including locally-sourced ingredients wherever possible. During the rest of the week there's a daily specials board. The pub is child-friendly and has a large car park and garden.

Opening times are 12 noon to 3 pm and 5.30 pm (6.30 pm on Saturday) to 11 pm on Monday to Saturday; 12 noon to 3 pm and 7 pm to 10.30 pm on Sunday. Food is served 12 noon to 2.30 pm Monday to Saturday and 12 noon to 3 pm on Sunday.

Telephone: 01767 313425.

The Walk

1 Walk along the right-hand side of the green along the High Street towards High Road, turning right at the top and following the houses round. Pass the Cock pub and the cottages on the left dedicated to local hero Janet Fordham and continue along the road as it swings to the right. The Cock is unusual in being a pub without a bar, with the beer coming straight up from barrels from the cellar. Just past some new houses a fingerpost signed to Biggleswade sends you to the left

and out into some fields. Follow the yellow-tipped marker posts, which direct you right across the field towards a small copse of trees. Continue in the same direction across the next field, which leads you to a corner and a gap in the hedge onto a road. Turn left and pick up the path on the other side of the road a few yards up.

2 You will now find yourself in a new field which you need to cross heading half-left, with the sign still directing you towards Biggleswade, whose church

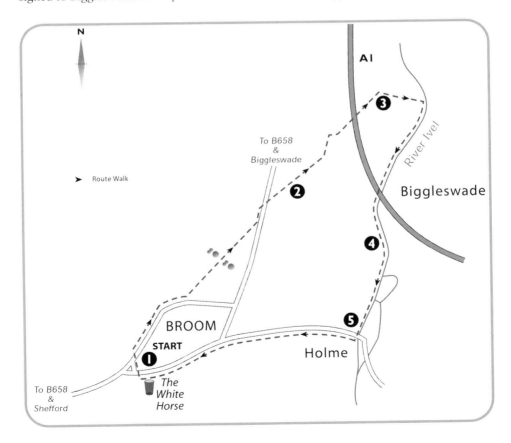

N

A1

To B658
&
Biggleswade

➤ Route Walk

River Ivel

Biggleswade

2

3

4

BROOM

5

START

1

Holme

To B658
&
Shefford

*The
White
Horse*

tower acts as a direction marker. You should head straight for the tower. This field is sometimes left to meadow and can be a seasonal haven for wildlife, in particular butterflies and birds. At a junction of paths turn right and over a small stream, following alongside it briefly, keeping the water on your left. On reaching a clearing you will be obliged to cross the busy dual carriageway of the A1 where you will need to take special care. On reaching the other side pick up the footpath once more.

The route winds its way alongside the River Ivel

3 You will now be joined by a rivulet on the right and another path joins from the left, but just keep aiming for the church tower. On reaching the River Ivel, where there's a small weir near an enclosed children's playground, turn right, keeping the water on your left. Before doing so it may be worth pausing to investigate Biggleswade itself, which retains many of its historic buildings. The river here is slow and languid and home to a variety of wildfowl. The peace hereabouts is broken only by the rush of traffic from the A1, but thankfully your second acquaintance with the road is via an underpass.

4 The river continues to pull you along with a few streams heading off to the left which once fed an ancient moat. The landmark these days along this stretch is Holme Mills, home to the Jordan's milling enterprise, and there is a small shop selling some of the company's goods which can be worth popping in on for sustenance or the occasional bargain. This is the last of the 450 independent flour mills that used to operate in Bedfordshire and it's also worth pausing here to take in the channel used to feed the mill.

5 Continue as if you'd turned right off the river path, going over the bridge and along the side of the road for about a mile until you come back into Broom. The fields along the side of the road were formerly used for harvesting onions and still grow market produce, with Broom itself once a centre for box-making. At one time the village supported four pubs, which were immortalised in the verse: 'The Black Horse, The White Horse, The Cock and The Plough, All met together and made a fine row!' You now pass the second of these on your left and will find yourself back at the green.

Place of Interest
The Swiss Garden, outside Old Warden to the west of Broom, is a compact example of an early 19th-century ornamental garden surrounding a romantic Swiss cottage. Rare trees combine with unusual architecture to make this a worthwhile visit. Telephone: 01767 627666.

Date walk completed:

The Pheasant Inn

capable of being physically turned to face the wind. Halfway round the walk there's another hill and the site of a farmhouse where the Great Train Robbers holed up immediately after their daring raid on the Night Mail. From this vantage point they could easily scan the roads below for tell-tale blue flashing lights.

This walk starts on the outskirts of the delightful village of Brill, a place awash with history sitting on top of the tallest of a range of hills on the Buckinghamshire/Oxfordshire border. The hill is capped, quite reasonably, by a windmill, a rare example of a 17th-century post mill, which means it is

The **Pheasant Inn** in Windmill Street is a friendly and unpretentious locals' pub, where there is an open fire in winter. On warmer days the garden affords spectacular views taking in seven counties as well as the windmill directly opposite. J.R.R. Tolkien and Roald Dahl both drank here. The extensive blackboard menu offers dishes from various cuisines with an emphasis on pasta and curry. As you might expect, the menus also usually includes pheasant in season. Beers include Young's and Hook Norton.

Distance: *4¹/₂ miles*

OS Explorer 180, Oxford, Witney and Woodstock
GR 653142

A moderate walk with some hilly parts; be prepared for patches of mud in the fields after rain

Starting point: The car park by the windmill in Brill.

How to get there: Brill lies a mile to the north-east of Oakley, which is on the B4011 between Thame and Bicester.

Opening times are 11 am to 3 pm and 5.30 pm to 11 pm on Monday to Saturday; 12 noon to 10.30 pm on Sunday. Closed on Christmas Day and Boxing Day. Lunch is served all week between 12 noon and 2 pm and evening meals between 7 pm and 9 pm.

Telephone: 01844 237104.

The Walk

1 Head away from the windmill down the lane marked 'South Hills' along the side of the pub, following the low wooden sign: 'Circular Walk'. On reaching a garage take the signpost for Leyhill, swinging left down a track. This then bends to the right and joins a pair of garages where you go over a stile. The footpath here runs between two hedges for a while before emerging onto open grassland. Aim slightly to the left where a stile brings you to the road.

2 Head right down the road and ignore the first footpath on your right, picking up instead the bridleway soon after. Pass down the cinder track for a short distance until you reach a stile. Cross this into a field and take a path heading half-right to a plank bridge and stile into the next field. The area around Brill used to have a number of brickworks and potteries and evidence of this industry can be found in the ploughed soil beneath your feet. Once over the stile follow the field boundary round to the left until you reach another stile in the corner. Cross this and turn

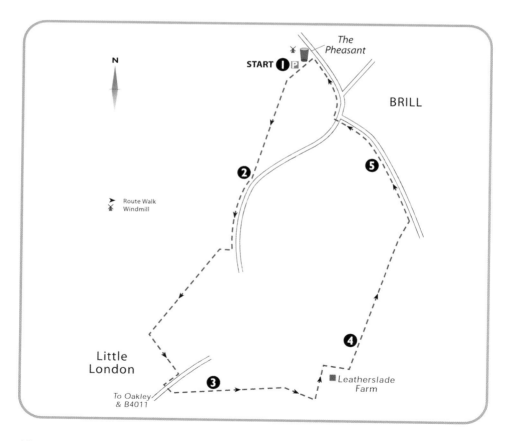

sharp left, heading for the cottages in front of you. You are now at the head of Little London Green. Follow the lane down to the road at the bottom and turn right. After a few yards, immediately opposite Little London Farm, there is another footpath over a field on the other side of the road. Take this and head half-left towards a metal gate.

3 Pass through the gate and head straight across the next field, aiming for the telegraph pole in front of you. The hedges hiding Leatherslade Farm are clearly visible on the hilltop and you need to aim for a gate slightly to its right. Although this is the site of the farm where the Train Robbers hid, the current building itself is more modern, its predecessor having been demolished. The path takes you round the edge of the property and when you reach the far corner in a small open space bear left and uphill through a warren of rabbit burrows bordered by trees. The going can be quite rough here, so take care.

4 The path eventually emerges at another metal gate which you go through, following the next field boundary on the right. Your climb should now be rewarded by more magnificent views to your left. Keep going along this path until you reach a corner, where there is a cut through to the road. Take this and turn left on reaching the road, following it back into Brill.

5 It is worth pausing to admire Brill as you pass through. Opposite the Red Lion just inside the village there's a fine Wesleyan chapel and some almshouses and a little further in, on the opposite side of the road, you will see some wonderful

The 17th-century post windmill at Brill

decorative brickwork and some intricate chimneys. On reaching the turn for Oakley by the green, bear right and stop to admire the public barometer set in the wall. This was erected in memory of Sir Edmund Verney of Claydon House in recognition of the service he provided for the people of Brill. The house opposite the barometer has an excellent wooden front door and sports an insurance plaque further up. Turn left down Windmill Street between the shops and this, unsurprisingly, returns you to the windmill and your car.

Place of Interest

The Boarstall Duck Decoy, on the west side of the B4011, is a rare example of a 17th-century decoy in working order and also offers a nature trail and exhibition hall. Opening times are restricted, so it is best to call first. Telephone: 01844 237488.

Date walk completed:

....

47

The Queen's Head

This steady walk offers an opportunity to approach one of the country's most impressive landscaped gardens by an unconventional route. Starting across fields, the tops of some of the follies within Stowe Park soon come into view and the streams feeding the lakes that are a feature of the park cut across the route. There is an option to pause the walk halfway round and tour the gardens, which are owned by the National Trust.

The **Queen's Head**, with its white façade is conveniently located near the car park. It is a splendid mix of village pub and restaurant, with an interesting menu to match. Particularly recommended are its ploughman's lunches, but there is a variety of food including rack of lamb with blackcurrant and mint sauce and halibut on a leek rosti. Refreshments are also available inside Stowe Park, where the tearooms offer ice cream from the local Beechdean Dairy.

Opening times at the Queen's Head are 12 noon to 3 pm and 6 pm to 11 pm (10.30 pm on Sunday). Food is served from 12 noon to 2 pm and 7 pm to 9 pm.

Telephone: 01280 813004.

Distance: *5¹/₄ miles*

OS Explorer 192 Buckingham and Milton Keynes
GR 687358

A steady walk across fields and along paths allowing an unconventional approach to Stowe Park

Starting point: The triangle of land at the village's western edge, where it is possible to leave your car.

How to get there: Chackmore is a mile north-west of Buckingham just off the A422.

The Walk

❶ Walk north from the Queen's Head up Main Street and past the school on your right. Just after the last of the houses take the footpath on your left and aim for the gate in the top right-hand corner of the field under an oak tree. In the next field take the path straight ahead until you reach a stile and plank bridge. Cross these and follow the right-hand boundary of the next field past the rusting farm machinery, which contrasts sharply with the scarlet pimpernel growing in the hedgerows in season.

❷ On approaching a track the first signs of Stowe Park appear in the shape of odd buildings and the house itself. Go through the gate on your right and head diagonally left (north-north-west) across the field, aiming for the gate ahead. The

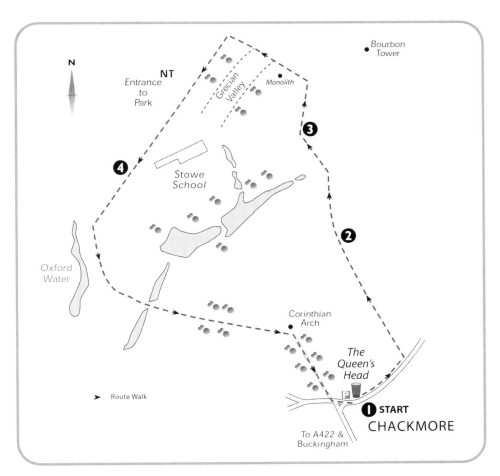

route goes under some telephone wires and through some short grass before cutting through a gap in the hedge and emerging onto open fields. Continue in the same direction until there is another gap in the hedge on the edge of the estate, marked by the imposing brick wall to your left. Go over the small stream feeding the lakes that lie beyond.

3 After another gate the path heads slightly left along a public footpath on National Trust property. Head uphill, looking out for monuments and follies either side of you, especially the Bourbon Tower on the hill ahead and to the right, which was originally a gatekeeper's lodge and now sports an octagonal tower. Aim for the monolith commemorating the Duke of Buckingham up above, moving away from the park's edge and merging with another path, keeping the sports ground of Stowe School to your right. The gate ahead of you comes out onto a long straight road and you need to turn left onto this.

You are now skirting the 'Grecian Valley' of the park, which was one of Capability Brown's very first commissions. The valley is overlooked by the two temples of Victory and Concord. The official entrance to the park lies about a third of the way along the road and there is an option to go into the park and take advantage of the beauty and facilities it offers.

Stowe Lake

4 Whether you go into the park or not, continue the walk along the straight road, going past the entrance to Stowe School. At the corner of the school grounds the path forks and you need to head left down towards a gate and a fingerpost pointing out over open ground. Keep the Oxford Water lake to your right and continue on the path which cuts through two of the park's other eight lakes. When the road divides slightly after this take the right-hand fork and go through some trees. The end of the path is marked by the imposing Corinthian Arch where there is a good view of the park behind you. Head downhill, keeping the arch behind you and turn left at the bend where rather unexpectedly you rejoin the car park.

Date walk completed:

....

Place of Interest

If **Stowe Park** isn't enough for you, **Sulgrave Manor** between Banbury and Northampton is not only the ancestral home of George Washington but also the headquarters of the Herb Society. The house is open on summer afternoons but is often booked for private functions or filming, so it is worth calling ahead first. Telephone: 01295 760205.

The George & Dragon

This is definitely a walk for a clear day, perhaps after visiting the windmill on a Sunday morning. Quainton Hill is one of the highest spots around and is not that difficult to conquer as the path follows a clear track to the top, with the effort involved in doing so well rewarded with magnificent views. The route is easy to follow and combines bridleways with minor roads and ends with the opportunity to wander around the pretty and historical village of Quainton.

The **George & Dragon** is a quintessential English village inn nestling between picturesque cottages. The saloon bar is divided by an impressive brick arch and there is a section in the pub for children which includes a chest of Lego.

Distance: 5$^1/_4$ miles

OS Explorer 192 Buckingham and Milton Keynes
GR 747202

A hilly walk, especially at the beginning, but well defined using bridleways

Starting point: The village green near the George & Dragon.

How to get there: Quainton lies 2 miles north of Waddesdon, which is on the A41 between Aylesbury and Bicester.

A wide selection of food is offered with specialities ranging from grills and steaks to vegetarian options. There's also a specials blackboard and a tempting selection of home-made sweets. OAP specials are available on Tuesday lunchtimes.

Opening times are 12 noon to 2.30 and 6 pm to 11 pm on Monday to Saturday; 12 noon to 3 pm and 7 pm to 10.30 pm on Sunday. Food is served from 12 noon to 2 pm and 6 pm to 9 pm on Tuesday to Saturday, as well as Monday evenings, and 12 noon to 2.30 pm on Sunday.

Telephone: 01296 655436.

The Walk

1 Quainton's windmill north of the triangular village green was built in 1830 from locally made bricks, and is open for viewing from 10 am to 1 pm every Sunday. The tallest windmill in the county, it needed to be this high because of its position in the lee of Quainton Hill. The green also has an unusual preaching cross and a useful information board. From here turn right along Church Road, following it as it bends round and picking up a footpath on the left opposite the Old School House. This takes you over a stile through a small field, with a gate in the top left-hand corner. Go through this and immediately Quainton Hill with its radio mast on top rises up before you.

2 Luckily, the ascent is broken into stages marked with a gate in the middle. Take the opportunity to pause here to reward yourself with the view of the Vale of Aylesbury behind you. Continue up the well-defined track to the top, passing to the left of the mast and reservoir, where a seat has thoughtfully been provided. Notice how small the windmill looks now and see if you can spot Waddesdon Manor in the distance. No such hill would be complete without a claim as to how far you can see from it, and in Quainton's case it is reputed that it's possible to see

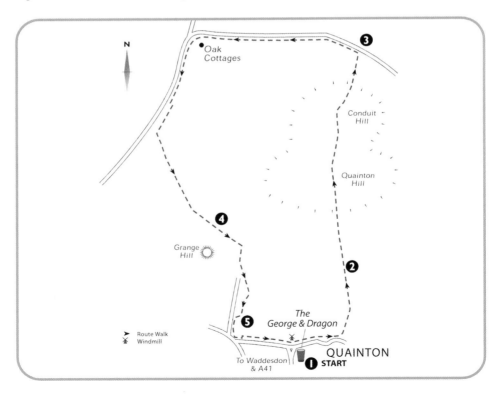

the Shropshire Hills from here. Pass over the peak of the hill where more great views await you. Continue with the track, passing through one gate and turning right after the second to pass down the side of Conduit Hill towards a farm. This dips down and leads to a gate and then a gap through the hedge. Continue to another gate and come out onto a farm track. Turn right and then left when you reach the lane by an attractive willow.

3 Continue on the road for just under a mile to Oak Cottages where you bear left and continue past one footpath until you reach another cutting across the road. Turn left here and then immediately right so you continue parallel to the road for a while along a cinder embankment. The path heads left after the next (rusty) gate and down some steps. Head out half-right across the field, aiming to pass to the left of the rising Grange Hill in front of you. Thankfully this hill does not have to be climbed, although the radio mast on Quainton Hill high on your left gives a reminder of what you've achieved already.

4 Pass through the kissing gate in front of you and follow the path to the left. On reaching a small line of trees at the base of the ridge coming off Grange Hill turn left, going over a pair of stiles, after which the path heads half-right for a gate. Go through this and select the path heading diagonally right across the field via a stile. Pass through a metal gate and along the path at the base of the hill, passing a pretty pond along the way.

5 Go through the gate at the bottom right-hand corner of the field and along the path past the back of some houses.

The preaching cross at Quainton with the windmill behind

You are now re-entering Quainton. Turn left at the road and then left again at the bottom, keeping left where the road forks to pass along Upper Street. Look out for the Quainton Parish Burials Acceptance stone lodged in the side of the verge on your left and keep going past the children's play area. The path continues to the top of the green and brings you back to your starting point.

Place of Interest

The award-winning **Buckinghamshire Railway Centre**, just south of Quainton, offers both full size steam engines and much to see in the recently-opened visitor centre. Trains are in steam every Sunday and bank holiday between March and October. Telephone: 01296 655720.

Date walk completed:

....

Long Crendon

The Chandos Arms

Mostly flat and easy, over a mixture of country roads and fields, this walk starts with extensive views across the Vale of Aylesbury and ends with a short trail around the historic village of Long Crendon. In between it cuts across open farmland and over a series of fresh spring streams. Originally a centre for lace making, Long Crendon also boasts the Old Courthouse, which was built as a wool store and is now in the care of the National Trust.

Perched on the edge of the village, the **Chandos Arms** has a welcoming old world ambience. The public bar, with its pool table, is bright and spartan, whilst the lounge bar has an open fireplace and an atmosphere conducive to dining. As such it is perfect after a long walk. In the summer the Devon cream teas can be tempting, whilst the home-made steak and kidney pie or local sausages with mashed potato and red wine and onion gravy are perfect after a good morning's ramble on a frosty day.

Opening times All day, although food is only served at lunchtimes.

Telephone: 01844 208669.

Distance: 5³/₄ miles

OS Explorer 180 Oxford, Witney and Woodstock
GR 688091

A flat walk along country roads and fields with a short steep climb towards the end

Starting point: The pub car park. Please obtain permission to leave your car while you walk.

How to get there: Long Crendon is on the B4011 between Thame and Oakley. If heading north, go through the village and down a hill; the pub is on the left.

The Walk

① Turn right out of the pub car park and head back towards the village until you reach the Angel Inn (these days more of a restaurant than a pub) where you turn right into Sandy Lane. Follow this as it curves first to the left and then to the right past Redding's Farm. Keep with the road at the junction with Frogmore Lane and strike out along the long straight stretch that follows, taking time to admire the views of the Vale of Aylesbury either side of you. Crest a small hill and then head

down. Shortly after an uncharacteristic kink in the road take the footpath on the left marked as the Thame Valley Walk, crossing over a stile into a field as you do so.

② Walk along the right-hand boundary of this field alongside the path of a spring stream. Cross the double stile at the end of the field (these stiles will shortly become a feature of this walk) and continue along the right-hand edge of the following field. Another pair of stiles with a plank bridge takes you into a third field where you stick

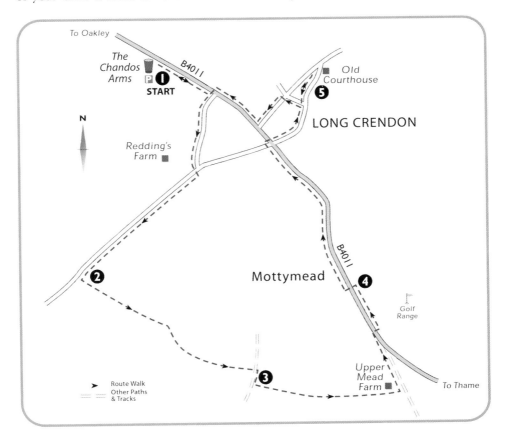

with the right-hand edge before it opens up. Follow the path straight ahead and slightly to the right, aiming for the edge of a hedge. On reaching the hedge follow the path slightly to the left across a field and at the opening in the boundary cut across the next field to a pair of stiles crossing an unmade track.

3 The footpath now bends to the right round the edge of the field until you reach yet another pair of stiles and a plank bridge over a stream. Continue over the next field following the left-hand boundary and follow this path over two more sets of stiles until you reach the now derelict Old Thame Road where you turn sharp left up the road. At Upper Mead Farm take the path straight ahead along the busier modern road, the B4011. The path crosses over this road near the Golf Range and shortly after the Bernwood Way, which has accompanied the Thame Valley Walk up until now, detours to the right.

4 The path crosses the road again at Mottymead and continues uphill into Long Crendon village, the last stage of the ascent being quite steep. At the crossroads in the village turn right (marked 'Village Roads Only'); this is the High Street and still part of the Thame Valley Walk. Your target is the Old Courthouse at the end of the street, and in getting there you may spot the old school house, the old police house, the old blacksmith's, the old chapel and the old bakery, giving a good feel for the past life of the village.

5 Head towards the church and on the left is the distinctively whitewashed building that is the Old Courthouse (see

The 15th-century courthouse at Long Crendon

below), which is well worth a visit. Pause by Madge (number 55) adjacent to the Eight Bells pub to admire the intricate brickwork and half-timbered exterior along with an exposed thatched courtyard entrance. Also note the blue plaque on the Old Church House marking the street party held to celebrate the Queen's Golden Jubilee in 2002, suggesting that the village remains a lively one! Retrace your steps and turn right down Butts Lane and then left at the crossroads. At the T-junction turn right and follow the road round until it reunites you with the pub.

Place of Interest

Long Crendon Courthouse, which is on the walk, is a 15th-century two-storey building that was used as the manorial courts from the reigns of Henry V to Victoria. It is open on Wednesday afternoons and from 11 am to 6 pm at weekends between April and September.

Date walk completed:

....

The Five Arrows

Perched on top of Lodge Hill, Waddesdon Manor provides the centrepiece for this fairly challenging stretch across fields and woodland, offering both a beacon and a goal, as well as a place to visit for culture and refreshment after the walk. Along the way the walk gives you extensive views across the Vale of Aylesbury as well as the opportunity to see a complex badger sett. The circuit starts and ends in the village

Distance: 5³/₄ miles

OS Explorer 181 Chiltern Hills North
GR 749169

Mainly footpaths across fields with some roads and the occasional steep hill

Starting point: There is a large layby to the east of the village.

How to get there: Waddesdon is 4 miles west of Aylesbury on the A41 to Bicester.

of Waddesdon, which alone is worth a visit to admire an impressive range of buildings within what is clearly still an active community.

The **Five Arrows,** passed at the end of the walk, boasts a club-style open foyer where visitors linger in deep leather chairs amongst velvet curtains reading the complimentary newspapers and *Country Life*. The menu demonstrates amply that this is no ordinary pub but rather a hotel with a kitchen to match. Diners may enjoy meals as diverse as smoked eel or braised lamb shank with port and rosemary sauce either here or in the large courtyard outside. A lunchtime specials board is always worth investigating. The Rothschild connection lingers with first growth clarets available from the estates in France, as well as champagne by the glass or, if you prefer, a pint of Fuller's or a guest beer.

Opening times are 11 am to 3 pm and 5.30 pm (6 pm on Saturday) to 11 pm on Monday to Saturday; 12 noon to 3 pm and 7 pm to 10.30 pm on Sunday. Food is served from 12 noon to 2.30 and 7 pm to 9.30 pm on Monday to Saturday; 12 noon to 2 pm and 7.30 pm to 8.30 pm on Sunday.

Telephone: 01296 651727.

The Walk

1 Take a left out of the parking area and follow the main road for 100 yards, picking up a footpath sign on the left heading towards some allotments. Walk through the gap between the vegetables and the stream until you come to a wide grass path on your left, which you need to follow until you reach a stile. Walk along the path on the other side as it goes round to the left, which describes the boundary of a school playing field, turning right and then right again, ignoring the path to the left as you approach some woods.

2 On reaching the woods the path bends first left then right through the trees. Follow this for 75 yards until you meet a path to the left over a stile. Cross the field on the other side, aiming to the right of a modern red brick house where there is a stile in the left-hand corner of the field. Cross this and pick up the metalled road, heading right until you reach a junction. Turn left here, passing through a wooden gate with footpath signs on the side. You should now be heading downhill along a long straight road. When the road finally bends, the path forks to the right over another stile and across a cultivated field.

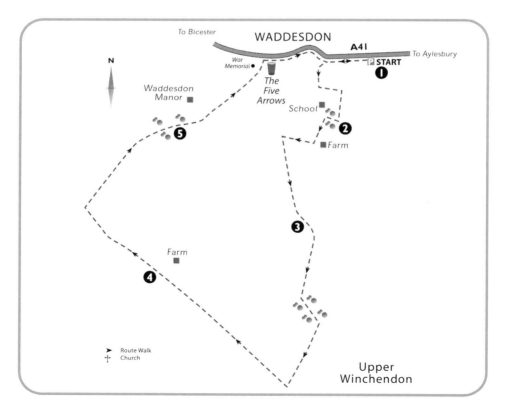

3 Pass through the beech coppice halfway across the field and then over another two fields connected by a gate, maintaining a southerly direction along clearly marked paths. In the subsequent pasture aim for the newly-planted run of trees crossing in front of you and walk between them, bearing right at the copse and metal fence protecting an ancient fish pond in a dip. Aim for the top left-hand corner of this area at the bottom of the manor house's garden, which in turn is just below the church. Cross the stile and maintain your direction, ignoring the path to Upper Winchendon. Behind you at this point are excellent views of the Vale of Aylesbury. The ground here can get quite muddy and uneven so take care. Aim for the left-hand corner of this open area where there is a stile and an intersection of paths, although there is a spectacular badger sett off to the right. Take the narrower concrete path to your right alongside the hedge leading downhill, and continue straight ahead for some distance.

4 Head half-left after the plank bridge (marked by a blue arrow) to keep the farm to your right. Towards the end of this long straight stretch you will begin to catch glimpses of the tips of Waddesdon Manor's towers above the trees on your right. You need to take the third footpath to your right, which comes after a gate and is distinguished by a yellow arrow marked 'Circular Walk'. This rises slowly and heads off half-right before entering some woods.

5 You are now entering the grounds of the Manor and the strange sounds you might hear are coming from the ornamental aviary behind the trees.

The fabulous Renaissance-style Waddesdon Manor

Follow the road round to the right and glimpse the Manor behind the trees. Some 100 yards before the ticket booths the path heads diagonally left and comes out into some open ground via a metal kissing gate. Cross the field and enter some more trees, following the clearly defined path past some garages until it emerges on a side road by a war memorial. Head for the main road and turn right, taking the chance to walk through this pretty village, defined by a range of architectural styles, not least that of the Five Arrows pub, as you make your way back to the starting point.

Place of Interest

Waddesdon Manor, to the south-west of the village, was built in the late 19th century by Baron Ferdinand de Rothschild to display his art collection. The house also has one of the finest Victorian gardens in Britain. Telephone: 01296 653211.

Date walk completed:

The Crooked Billet

It's hard to believe that Milton Keynes was once a village but this walk through one of the few remaining small villages on the edge of that city provides an opportunity to imagine what it might have been like. The route starts with part of the Milton Keynes Boundary Walk and soon provides a glorious view of the distant village of Newton Longville. Using a local cycleway it doubles back on itself before a trek through a series of pastures returns to the starting point.

The Crooked Billet acts both as the village local and a superior restaurant. Bar meals can range from bubble and squeak fishcake with poached egg through to ciabatta snacks. The restaurant's à la carte menu on the other hand may include roasted turbot with lobster mash. Booking ahead is advisable.

Opening times are 12 noon to 2.30 pm and 5.30 pm to 11 pm on Monday to Saturday; 12 noon to 4 pm and 7 pm to 10.30 pm on Sunday. Food is served on Tuesday to Sunday between 12 noon and 2 pm and in the evenings. The Crooked Billet is closed during the first two weeks of January and on 25th/26th December.

Telephone: 01908 631979.

Distance: *6 miles*

OS Explorer 192 Buckingham and Milton Keynes
GR 843315

A combination of field paths, tracks and roads with some steady gradients

Starting point: The car park of the Crooked Billet (with landlord's permission).

How to get there: Newton Longville is 2 miles south-west of Bletchley and can be reached via the A421 to Buckingham or the A4146 to Leighton Buzzard.

The Walk

1 Head down the track opposite Westbrook End, signed to Hammond Park, crossing over a series of stiles and keeping to the left-hand edge of a patch of open ground. Cross over a wooden bridge near a tree burnt out by lightning and then go through a bridge under a disused railway, after which the route follows the left-hand edge of a large cultivated field.

After a steady climb uphill you reach a track at the corner of the field where you turn left and walk south-west along the curiously named Weasel Lane. The views to the left are of Newton Longville where you started.

2 Just past an attractive white house cross the road and continue along the track, now marked as a cycleway (number 51) to Winslow. The track eventually

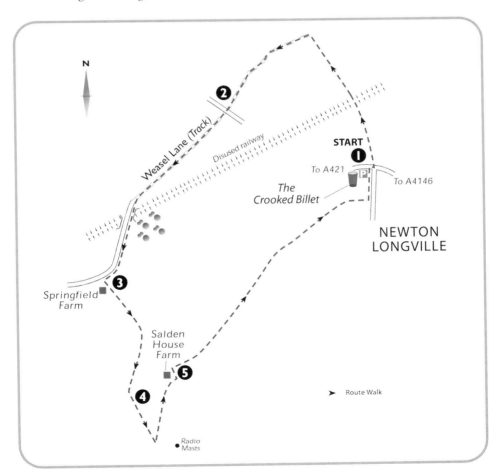

leads to the house that shares its name with the road, Weasels Lodge, with the track passing right by the front of the house. On reaching a T-junction at the end of the drive bear left and cross a bridge going over the railway you met earlier. The track now becomes metalled and bears slightly uphill. Salden Wood on the left of the road gives a lovely display of bluebells in the late spring.

③ Sandwiched between a bungalow and Springfield Farm, look for a path heading left through a gate and then a gap in the wooden fence beyond – aim for the gap on the right as there are two. Continue through a rusted metal gate in front of you and aim for the large farm in the distance, keeping by the hedge on your left. At the end of the field go over the stile and maintain your direction on the resulting track, moving into a field at a stile where the track has a spur to the right. Maintain your direction and follow the signs until you reach another metal gate in the top right-hand corner.

④ The path splits here and you need to turn to the left, following the rough track once again along the left-hand boundary of a field, making sure you keep the water tower on your right. Cross the stile in the corner of the field and after the next stile turn left over another stile into a large open pasture with radio masts on your right. It is from here that you can see Milton Keynes on the horizon. Head downhill, aiming for the bottom left-

Newton Longville seen from across the fields

hand corner of the field where you emerge onto a concrete road.

⑤ Turn left and continue on this road to the farm gate where there is a stile on your right. Cross this and turn left at the lake and then half-right at the stile over another field. In the top corner there is yet another stile, and the path doubles back and leads you onto a large crop field via a small metal gate. The path here is very well defined and keeps you on a steady north-east passage for $1\frac{1}{2}$ miles. On finally reaching the field's edge cross the stile and then a series of small pastures which eventually bring you out onto a road. Turn left here and continue through the village back to your starting point.

Date walk completed:

....

Place of Interest
Bletchley Park, to the north, provides an opportunity to delve into the fascinating history of early computers and how they were used to crack Nazi codes during the Second World War. Telephone: 01908 640404.

The Robin Hood

of the first half of the walk. Field walking is a feature of the remainder of the circuit.

A sign at the road junction states that the **Robin Hood** is 359 paces away, and you may want to test this out as you approach this charming 17th-century pub in the heart of the village. The two bars offer different degrees of comfort, with the lounge opening out onto a practical wooden conservatory and a pleasant secluded garden. The walls have photos of actors who have played the 'man in green', but it's not recorded if any have ever sampled the chef's own steak and kidney pie or chilli beef pasta. If they had, they may have followed with the splendid Edinburgh cheesecake (topped with raspberries soaked in whisky) or citrus lemon and lime torte.

An easy stroll with one or two sharp drops but some glorious scenery, taking in the meadows which the poet William Cowper and the Reverend John Newton used as the inspiration for many of their poems and hymns. The path follows an ancient trade route and as such is well marked, with the spire of St Peter and St Paul in Olney a landmark for most

Distance: *3¹/₂ miles*

OS Explorer 207 Newport Pagnell and Northampton South
GR 903512

Mostly flat across meadows with one or two short sharp inclines. Some muddy patches after wet weather so wear good boots!

Starting point: The Robin Hood. Park in the main road going through Clifton Reynes.

How to get there: Clifton Reynes is just east of the A509 between Olney and Newport Pagnell.

Opening times are 12 noon to 3 pm and 6.30 pm to 11 pm on Tuesday to Saturday (closed all day Monday); 12 noon to 3 pm and 7 pm to 10.30 pm on Sunday. Food is served 12 noon to 2 pm each lunchtime and 7 pm to 9.30 pm Tuesday to Saturday. No food is available Sunday evening.

Telephone: 01234 711574.

The Walk

1 Turn left out of the pub and continue up the road to the church gates where you bear left and head slightly uphill past the magnificent Old Rectory to a point where the road runs out. Do not proceed up the track but rather pass through the kissing gate on your right, noting, and heading towards, the distant spire of St Peter and St Paul in Olney. Head half-left across a field, keeping the church to your right.

2 At the other end of the field cross over a stile and head downhill to the right, following a well-trodden path. On reaching a clearing in the hedge bear even more to the right and head steeply downhill, aiming for the river. The path is marked by a series of paving stones and emerges onto a pair of bridges taking you over the pretty River Great Ouse, which runs in a series of streams at this point. Cross the river and head straight for the church using a path that starts in concrete but soon becomes a field path, which in turn passes over a charming wooden footbridge across one of the many nearby streams.

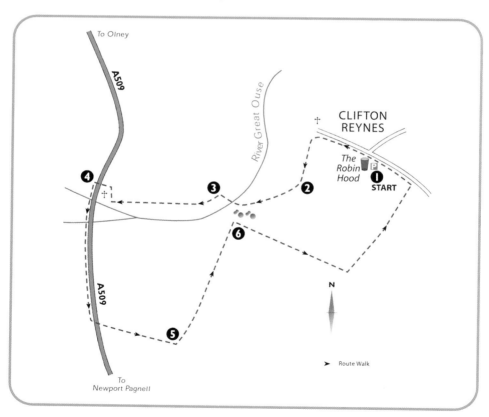

3 Continue heading for the church, although it is worth taking in the view of the reed-lined banks to your left. The Old Mill and weir, guarded by a majestic willow, now make an appearance and you need to aim to the right of them down a path that funnels between the mill and some cottages via a gate and a stile and then bears right and slightly uphill alongside the church. On reaching the churchyard take the entrance on your left and pass by the church's entrance and a splendid steel flagpole.

The Old Mill and weir

4 On reaching the junction with the main road turn left and cross over the river again using two bridges, the second of which has a weir to the right. Cross over a third bridge and on reaching a fourth pick up the footpath just before it on the left on the other side of the road using the stile. The church is now firmly on your left. Pass the cattle trough and cross a plank bridge over a dry stream on the right, climbing over the resulting fence and turning left into a field of sheep. Keep the field boundary to your left and cross over the stile 20 yards along the boundary after the corner.

5 The path now heads half-right across a field and you need to aim for the top right-hand corner. From here the path crosses over another field and you should aim for a gate, passing over a pair of old railway sleepers bridging a ditch. On reaching the gate, cross over and head for the trees straight in front of you. Stick to the right of them and, on arriving at a wooden fence, head uphill for 20 yards to a stile where you cross over and continue straight ahead towards a line of horse chestnut trees.

6 Turn right at these and cross the stile in front of you. Continue in the same direction in the next field, ignoring the path to your left. This cuts across the heart of the field slightly to the right of some telephone wires and ends up at yet another stile. Cross this and follow the path across the centre of another field and on reaching a telegraph pole head left as indicated, aiming for the top left-hand corner. This then emerges into a road where you turn left, back to the pub.

Place of Interest

The Cowper and Newton Museum in Olney covers not just these two poets but also the history of Olney right back to the Ice Age. The accent is, however, on the two men after whom the museum is named, who were responsible for *Amazing Grace* amongst other works. The museum is closed during the winter and on Mondays. Telephone: 01234 711516.

Date walk completed:

....

The Three Locks

Both canal and river bring different elements to this walk, which starts by winding along the floor of the Ouzel valley and then climbs one side of it to allow the walker to gain a completely different perspective of the local topography. The charming village of Great Brickhill offers an opportunity to pause halfway round and on the final stretch the canal offers its own set of delights.

The **Three Locks** sits right on the edge of the water and is the perfect place to indulge in 'gongoozling' or looking at canal-folk as they go about their business. The menu offers light bites such as burgers and jacket potatoes, as well as a kids' menu, through to more substantial offerings such as Hawaiian and Cajun chicken and chilli con carne and vegetarian options.

Opening times are 12 noon to 11 pm on Monday to Saturday; 12 noon to 10.30 pm on Sunday. Food is served from 12 noon to 9 pm on Monday to Saturday and 12 noon to 5 pm on Sunday.

Telephone: 01525 270592.

Distance: *5³/₄ miles*

OS Explorer 192 Buckingham and Milton Keynes
GR 891282

A gradual climb up the side of a valley but the beginning, middle and end are all flat and easy

Starting point: The layby alongside the Three Locks pub.

How to get there: The Three Locks is on the A4146 a mile south of Stoke Hammond and 3 miles to the north of Linslade.

The Walk

❶ Head north on the towpath, away from the locks, leaving the pub behind you. Don't worry, it's not going anywhere and should still be there for you when you get back. Before long, there's a ground level marker on the left stating that the canal centre of Braunston is 42 miles away, and these markers are useful milestones (quite literally) whether you're walking or afloat. Cross over the first bridge and pick up the towpath again,

passing the old swingbridge and Stoke Hammond Lock, where the canal falls 7 feet. You are joined at this point by the River Ouzel and there is a run off from the canal into the river about 10 feet below.

❷ On reaching the second mile marker leave the towpath, going through a small gap and up some steps before turning right onto a minor road. Do not go past bridge 102. The walk now follows part of the Milton Keynes Boundary Walk, although the metropolis seems a long

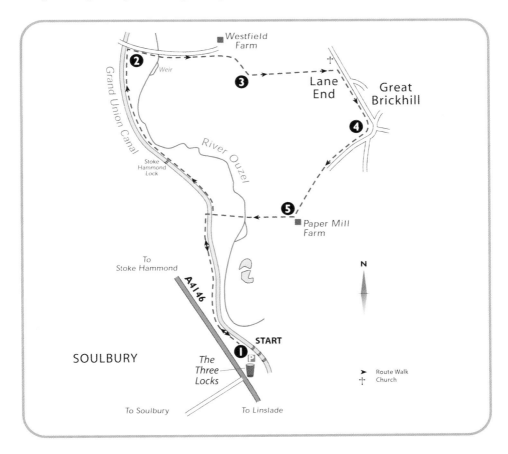

way away. A series of three stone bridges takes you over branches of the Ouzel, which can be heard tumbling over a number of small weirs as well as a more significant waterfall, visible from the third of the three bridges. The path then diverts to the right opposite the road leading up to Westfield Farm. Cross the field in front of you diagonally to the right until you reach the boundary on the other side, marked by a small wood planted in 2002 to mark the Queen's Golden Jubilee.

❸ On reaching the corner of the field turn left, keeping the derelict wall alongside you. This leads to a disused gateway where you bear right at the wooden fence, marked by a line of trees. Go over the stile at the top of the field and then up a narrow track, which brings you to a road where you turn left. On reaching the war memorial turn right, which brings you into Lower Way in Great Brickhill where there is an impressive curved wooden front door in one of the houses. Keep on this road, past Chartwell Moor, staying on the pavement until it runs out.

❹ The path curves to the right at the Old Red Lion pub and falls into Ivy Lane. The impressive Cromwell Cottages, with a weaving of thatch covering their roof, are on the opposite side of the road. Bear right almost immediately into Stoke Lane, joining the public bridleway with Broomhill House on the left. At Haines Farm follow the track to the left and downhill through some trees where the path can become quite muddy, so be careful.

❺ As you approach the bottom of the hill the gurgling of water from the various streams hereabouts becomes more

THE THREE LOCKS

prominent and on reaching Paper Mill Farm turn right onto an unmade road. One of those small streams runs to your left and its destination soon becomes obvious as two bridges appear over the Ouzel. The road leads you back to the bridge you crossed earlier when changing towpath. To return to the pub simply go back over the bridge and retrace your steps for about a mile.

Place of Interest

The Leighton Buzzard Railway offers a 70-minute journey along a narrow gauge railway that dates back to the First World War. Notable for its steep gradients and tight corners, the railway runs a number of theme days. Telephone: 01525 373888.

Date walk completed:

....

The Lions of Bledlow

This walk celebrates two highways from different eras sharing the same name. The first is the Icknield Way, which straddles a ridge along the county border and offers some spectacular views, whilst the second is the Icknield Line, a branch railway now thriving after a period of inactivity. The latter's route is clearly visible from the former, as is the ever-present Whiteleaf Cross, a chalk monument which acts as a landmark throughout. The walk starts in the tucked away village of Bledlow, whose picturesque qualities are born out by the fact that it is a popular TV location, having featured in a number of episodes of *Midsomer Murders*.

The **Lions of Bledlow** is unusual, and possibly unique, in having two lions in its sign rather than the more usual three. The building is something of a Tardis inside, with a warren of rooms. The low-beamed ceilings verge on the hazardous but there's room to stand on the quarry tiles around the three-quarter sided bar or next to the massive fireplace. Outside there's more seating in the garden or on the green, a perfect place to while away a summer's Sunday afternoon. Food ranges from filled baguettes to the more adventurous such as tuna steak in Cajun spices or Barbary duck.

Opening times are 12 noon to 3 pm (with food until 2.30 pm) and 6 pm to 11 pm (food until 9.30 pm, 9 pm on Sundays).

Telephone: 01844 343345.

Distance: *5¹/₄ miles*

OS Explorer 181 Chiltern Hills North GR 776021

A mix of road and fieldside walking with one steep hill at the beginning

Starting point: In the pub car park (with the owner's permission).

How to get there: Bledlow is ¹/₂ mile south of the B4009 halfway between Chinnor and Princes Risborough.

The Walk

❶ Turn left out of the car park and up an unmade track. Ignore the sign tempting you to the right to Chinnor Reserve and stride on up the hill straight ahead. Through gaps in the trees on the left you can gain the first of many sightings of the Whiteleaf Cross in the hillside opposite. This pull uphill makes for a vigorous start to the walk, but it's soon over and worth it in the end. The Icknield Way crosses over in front of the path at the top of the hill and here you turn right along a gloriously even and relatively flat path.

❷ The route now falls gently off the ridge, offering the occasional snatched view to the right through trees. It is worth glancing upwards too, to see if you can catch a glimpse of one of the red kites recently reintroduced here. On meeting some housing and a profusion of signs turn right, signposted 'Swan's Way', but pause to catch the view from this vantage point first. After 50 yards take the path over a stile on your left where you swap one expansive view for another, this time towards Wainhill Spring and the Icknield railway line. Pass along the left-hand side of the field

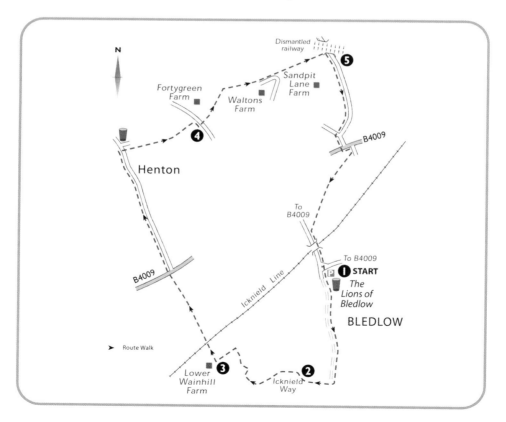

heading steadily downhill and pick up the path on your left through the hedge.

❸ On emerging from a fenced-in section turn immediately right before Lower Wainhill Farm, aiming directly for the railway. Take special care crossing the tracks and continue straight ahead on the other side until you reach the road (Lower Icknield Way). Cross over and turn right and then left towards Henton, a village made up of a confusion of building styles, old and new. Continue along the road until it begins to peter out, taking the path leading to, and then to the right of, the pretty Peacock Hotel. When the buildings run out cut half-right across the next field before crossing the well-hidden plank bridge and stiles near the top left-hand corner. Cut half-right again over the next field, aiming for Fortygreen Farm via a metal gate.

❹ On reaching the road turn right and then left, picking up a fresh path. Continue until you reach an intersection where you keep going straight ahead in an adjacent field via two stiles. In the last field before Waltons Farm head half-right towards a metal gate in the corner. Turn right after the stile and then over another onto a road. Where this bends go through the metal gate and take the right-hand path, passing through the farm machinery on the other side and over another plank bridge. Keep going through a metal gate and aim for the attractive yellow house. The house to the left of this used to be the station on this disused stretch of railway, now a cycle route.

❺ Turn right along the road and continue until the crossroads where you cross straight over into Perry Lane. After

A marvellous view along the Icknield Way

50 yards there's a footpath on your right down the edge of an old brick cottage. Follow this along a stream, keeping straight ahead after a metal gate to another gate after which you turn left then right towards some trees, walking between two fields and rejoining the stream. Stay with the water across a paddock over further stiles until you eventually reach a road where you turn left. This takes you under the Icknield Line one last time, carried above you on a bridge, before returning you to the pub.

Place of Interest
The Chinnor and Princes Risborough Railway in Chinnor, just south-west of Bledlow, was formed ten years ago by enthusiasts to keep this typical country branch line open. Both diesel and steam trains are run but it's best to call ahead to the talking timetable first to check when and where. Telephone: 01844 353535.

Date walk completed:

....

The Stag & Huntsman

Hambleden has the look of a place stuck in a time warp. Even its garage seems more 1950s than 21st century. It's not surprising therefore that film and TV producers have been drawn to it, with Disney's *101 Dalmatians* and ITV's *As Time Goes By* and *Midsomer Murders* amongst its credits. The walk takes you through the village and up into magnificent beech woods. A few climbs are rewarded with extraordinary views, including the valley below and one of the Thames. Look up and you may catch a glimpse of a red kite, recently reintroduced to the area.

The **Stag & Huntsman** on the edge of the village is a 400-year-old traditional brick and flint inn, offering an extensive menu of wholesome pub grub ranging from an awe-inspiring mixed grill through pies to vegetarian curries, taking in the ever popular ploughman's on the way. There is an extensive garden, and a crisp modern restaurant.

Opening times are 11 am to 2.30 pm (3 pm on Saturday) and 6 pm to 11 pm Monday to Saturday; 12 noon to 3 pm and 7 pm to 10.30 pm on Sunday. Meals are served from 12 noon to 2 pm and 7 pm to 9.30 pm on Monday to Saturday; 12 noon to 2 pm on Sunday. Closed on Christmas Day.

Telephone: 01491 571227.

Distance: *6¹/₂ miles*

OS Explorer 171 Henley on Thames and Wallingford
GR 785865

A reasonably ambitious walk with a few steep climbs

Starting point: There is a free public car park behind the pub.

How to get there: Hambleden lies a mile north of the A4155 midway between Henley and Marlow.

The Walk

1 Head towards the centre of the village, leaving the pub behind you. Pass the war memorial and lychgate and cross the Hamble Brook. On reaching the road, cross over and head uphill using the metalled path in front of you. A short but steep climb takes you into a beech wood where there is plenty of evidence of storm damage. At the crest of the hill pause to take in the view of the Thames below you and then bear right, taking the path into the woods.

2 Go straight ahead into the heart of the wood. You are now walking along a ridge and can enjoy glimpses of the view below

either side. At the summit of the hill there's a small clearing where you head slightly right, still keeping to the path. This becomes a vehicle track and soon emerges into an open area and a plantation. Keep going straight, ignoring other tracks, until there is a clear junction where the woods begin to thin ahead and to your right. The path now takes you through a clearly defined route between two lines of trees. After a short climb you reach a footpath, clearly marked on a tree as HA42. Go straight ahead, back into the woods.

3 The path now heads downhill and becomes very distinct, with magnificent views of the Great Wood to your left.

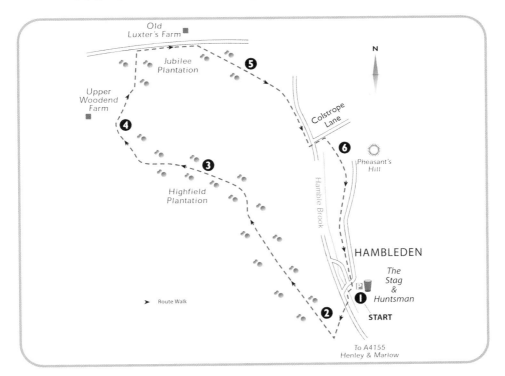

73

Skirt the edge of Highfield Fir Plantation and where the path meets another coming from the left, dog-leg in order to maintain your previous direction (due west), so that you are now heading uphill, leading up to the left-hand edge of the wood. The path here is clearly marked. Follow it until it meets a ditch and, later, the edge of the wood, with a field opening up on your left.

4 Just before you reach Upper Woodend Farm watch out for a footpath crossing over in front of you, which is easily missed. Take this to the right, over the first stile of the walk, and cut across the field in front of you. Keep to the left-hand edge of the pasture in the next field until you reach the edge of another wood. At its first corner there is another stile. Follow this and head straight ahead until you reach a single-track tarmac road. Take this to the right and when you reach Old Luxters Farm (see Places of Interest) bear right into the Jubilee Plantation of beech trees.

5 You now begin the descent off the ridge, with seats thoughtfully provided to allow you to contemplate what you have already walked. A dedicated bench marks the spot where the woods give way to an open hill looking out over the Hambleden valley with a steep fall to a road, the path passing through a hedge on the way. Turn right at the road and follow it until you reach Colstrope Lane. Go down this and after 50 yards take the footpath on the right, going over a couple of stiles and an unusual wooden staired stile.

6 Cross the field and go over another stile, turning right at a T-junction of paths and head for the red brick house, passing

An attractive wooden staired stile

through a pair of kissing gates. Go down the side of the house and over the driveway to a path leading down the backs of some gardens with a view of the Hamble Brook on your right. The path continues just below the road with the church acting as a landmark in front of you. Halfway through the last field the path joins the road on the left, leading you back into the village and your car, going past a series of brick and flint cottages and the birthplace of Lord Cardigan, the man who led the charge of the Light Brigade.

Place of Interest

Chiltern Valley Winery and Brewery at Old Luxters Farm, which is on the walk, offers the full 'grape to glass' experience. Wine has been produced here for over 20 years and visitors (who must book ahead: 01491 638330) not only get to see behind the scenes but also enjoy a sampling session including both wines and beers.

Date walk completed:

The Le de Spencers Arms

An undulating walk mainly through woods offering spectacular views across the Chiltern Hills as well as the opportunity to visit Disraeli's Hughenden Manor. Bluebells and wood anemones provide a carpet of colour around springtime. Towards the end of the walk the trees part to offer a glimpse of the yellow façade of West Wycombe

House, recognisable as the location for the recent film *The Importance of Being Earnest*, as well as its distinct mausoleum. The Le de Spencers Arms halfway round is one of Wycombe's best-kept secrets and the perfect place to stop whatever the season.

The oldest building on Downley's ancient common, the brick and flint **Le de Spencers Arms** is named after the family who used to own the local estate. Hidden away well down a small track, the pub has its own car park and garden and visitors are welcome alongside a hardcore of locals and Wycombe cognoscenti. Low beams and aged wooden panelling complement furnishings that give the pub a 'lived in' look. A popular venue for local musicians, the pub also holds regular special events and occasional beer festivals. The menu is simple but honest, ranging from snacks to grills, and includes an all day breakfast

Distance: 5 miles

OS Explorer 172 Chiltern Hills East
GR 847969

Some steep gradients but mainly firm underfoot

Starting point: Naphill village hall car park.

How to get there: Naphill lies west of the A4128 between High Wycombe and Great Missenden. The village hall is adjacent to a large playing field on the main road straight through the village.

Opening times are 12 noon to 3 pm and 6 pm to 11 pm on Monday to Friday and all day at weekends. Meals are served daily from 12 noon to 2 pm (roasts on Sunday) and on Friday and Saturday evenings, although a phone call ahead may secure food outside these times.

Telephone: 01494 535317.

The Walk

1 From the car park turn right onto the pavement and walk alongside the playing field until you reach a bend in the road just after a small grocery. Go down Church Lane straight ahead, which becomes a track after a gate, and follow the path as it swings left downhill into the woods marking the beginning of the Hughenden Estate. Pass through the car park and bear slightly left downhill at a fork. The road becomes metalled here and meets a T-junction, where there is an excellent view out over open grazing. Turn right, going uphill past the entrance to the Manor. Continue straight ahead through the woods on a bridleway marked 'Boundary Walk'.

2 At the bottom of the hill the path emerges onto open fields. Follow this

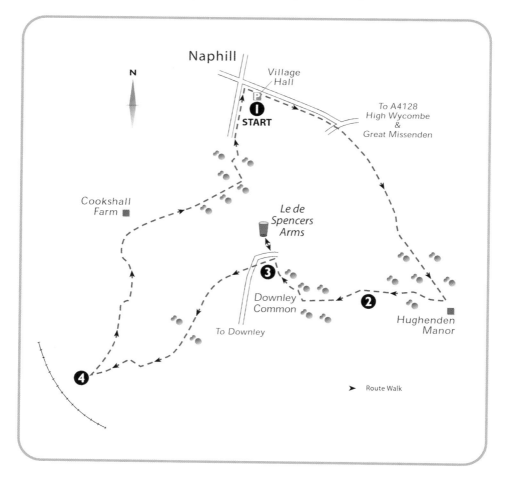

through various twists and turns until you enter some more woods. Continue through these up a gentle gradient and bear slightly left at the junction with a number of paths. Notice the abundance of flints underfoot which are used in the local housing. The woods hereabouts have a number of deep pits where the flint used to be mined and these can prove hazardous for walkers! Pass Well Cottage, walking along the gravel driveway until you reach another junction where you turn right past a church. Head up the steep slope and cut across the common and the scorched earth that marks the site of the annual bonfire on 5th November.

The old blacksmith's forge at Downley

❸ The path emerges onto a road. Where it bends continue straight ahead and then left down an unmade track to the Le de Spencers Arms. Retrace your steps after taking your refreshment and follow the road round the side of the playing field until you reach a path sandwiched between an old blacksmith's forge (now used to store cricket equipment) and a flint cottage. Follow this path downhill, looking out for West Wycombe House in the distance on your left. Just before the railway, take the road that doubles back behind you to the north-east, taking in the view of the West Wycombe Mausoleum.

❹ This road continues for nearly a mile, offering an excellent vista of the valley of the Wye behind you. Just before Cookshall Farm take the path to the right into some birch and beech trees and continue straight ahead past some pines until you reach a stile. Cross this and the field the other side to enter a last set of woods, where you turn immediately left and then right at the next junction. After 30 yards turn left and then right until you emerge onto an unmade road. Follow this round the corner by a pond and turn right where it meets the main road, where you will renew acquaintance with the village hall at Naphill.

Date walk completed:

....

Places of Interest
Hughenden Manor, on the walk, was the home of Benjamin Disraeli for over 30 years. Now a National Trust property, the house and gardens are open some weekdays and weekends from March to October; phone ahead for details 01494 755565. **West Wycombe Park**, which along with the village that bears its name is also part of the National Trust, offers more restricted opening times, but the park, littered with follies, is worth a visit. Telephone: 01494 513569.

The Pink & Lily

A pleasant and un-demanding stroll through woodland taking in one of the area's most famous pubs as well as the opportunity to connect with history ranging from the Iron Age through the Civil War to the Great War. Well-defined paths make it difficult to get lost and towards the end of the walk there's a magnificent viewpoint across the Chiltern Hills.

The **Pink & Lily** is well known for its connections with the war poet Rupert Brooke, who often drank here and even composed verses in and about the pub. A 'snug' with polished oak panelling is devoted to his memory and, it seems, to the equally serious business of the hostelry's dominoes and cribbage teams. The pub is one of the highest in the Chilterns and takes its food and drink seriously. Six real ales are on offer and food can be ordered from a basic menu, the specials board or the 'Something Different' menu, which includes delights such as quail breast salad or smoked duck. The non-smoking colonial-style conservatory offers a convivial spot to eat, but there are other bars and also a small garden.

Distance: $4^1/_2$ miles

OS Explorer 181 Chiltern Hills North
GR 827019

Relatively flat with few stiles but can be muddy in places

Starting point: The car park of the Pink & Lily pub (with permission) or the layby opposite.

How to get there: Lacey Green lies to the east of the A4010 between West Wycombe and Princes Risborough. The start point is a mile down the road in Parslow's Hillock at the northern end of the village, the turn marked by the Whip pub.

Opening times are 11 am to 11 pm on Monday to Saturday and 11 am to 6 pm on Sunday. Meals are served at lunchtime every day and in the evenings on Monday to Saturday.

Telephone: 01494 488308.

The Walk

1 Set off down the metalled Lily Bottom Lane by the side of the pub for around ¼ mile until you reach a footpath by the attractive Iron Beech Cottage. Turn left and pick up the path on the other side of the cottage, heading right along the edge of some woods. Continue just inside the wood for ½ mile until you reach an obvious junction marked by a wooden fence. Turn left here into the heart of the woods, with the footpath running parallel to the bridleway. The path ends with a dip down to a crossroads where you pick up another directly opposite, off the road heading to Hughenden.

2 Follow the path marked with a white cross which heads left and stick with it, ignoring branches off to the right. A stile brings you out onto a cricket pitch with the pretty yellow walls of the Hampden Arms (01494 488255) providing a distinctive landmark on the other side. At the crossroads cut straight across onto a gravel drive, which leads to a footpath between two garages. Take this, passing through a kissing gate, pausing only to notice the curious modern folly at the bottom of the garden of the house on your right. Cut straight across an open cultivated field and follow the left-hand edge of the grazing that follows until it comes to a gate by a wooded pond. Pass through this and head for the flint church.

3 Pass to the left of the church of St Mary Magdalene and come out in front of Hampden House with its impressive chimneys. The family of John Hampden, who led a rebellion against the ship tax of

Charles I and contributed to the unrest that led to the Civil War, lived on this site from 1066 to the 18th century. There is a monument to John Hampden about a mile to the east of the walk and he is buried in the church. Today the house and estate are in private hands. Pass by the front of the offices on your left and pick up the Chiltern Way by a gate, sticking to the right-hand side of the field until it ducks into the edge of the woods. The path now follows the base of part of Grim's Ditch, the network of ditches and banks across Southern Britain, parts of which date back to the Iron Age, although no one quite knows what it is for.

4 At the end of the field the path dog-legs to re-enter woodland. Continue straight ahead, with Grim's Ditch passing in front of you, along the bridleway or footpath alongside it. The path here is marked with white arrows on trees and you follow it until an intersection with a vehicle track. Head right, following a dip down then up again until you reach an intersection by open land. Turn left here and proceed just inside the edge of the wood until you come to some houses. Head down the short drive and turn left by the post box along a road.

5 After 200 yards pick up a path to the right, again following the edge of some woods. Follow this path left then half-right, ignoring the track heading downhill. You will pass an excellent viewpoint across the Chilterns and eventually emerge on a short track at the back of some houses. Take this left and then turn right on the road where you will see the Pink & Lily once again. You will notice that the pub stands at the

The 17th-century smockmill at Lacey Green

crossroads of Pink Road and Lily Bottom Lane and presumably this is how the pub got its name. A more romantic theory, however, is that the pub was opened by a Mr Pink, the butler at Hampden House, who married a Miss Lily, a parlour maid at the same house.

Places of Interest

Lacey Green Windmill (open Sundays from May to September and bank holidays), just to the south of the start point, is a 17th-century smock mill, so called because of its appearance, and is the oldest example of its type still standing. Telephone: 01844 343560. **Whiteleaf Hill** to the east of Princes Risborough is also worth visiting for its butterflies and wildflowers native to the chalk downs, as well as the recently restored chalk cross and panoramic views.

Date walk completed:

....

Butlers Cross 25 Walk

The Russell Arms

of Chequers, where you need to be prepared to have your movements monitored by CCTV, and closes with a sweep down past a curious geological feature known as Ellesborough Warren towards the local church sitting proudly on a mound.

The **Russell Arms** in Chalkshire Road, just across the road from the village hall, is named after the family that once owned Chequers and is a rendered brick and flint cottage of two parts. The first is a rustic but welcoming public bar which itself is divided into an oak-beamed parlour and a bar food area lined with old stone jars and bottles. The second is a light and airy restaurant decorated on more modern lines. There is food to suit every taste from club sandwiches, filled baguettes, liver and bacon, and herb sausages, to more exotic dishes such as baked sea bass, linguine and Italian-style lamb shank.

Opening times are 11.30 am to 3 pm and 6 pm to 11 pm on Monday to Saturday; 12 noon to 3 pm and 7 pm to 10.30 pm on Sunday. Food is served on Monday to Saturday from 12 noon to 2 pm and 7 pm to 9.30 pm and on Sunday from 12 noon to 4 pm (no food available Sunday evening).

Telephone: 01296 622618.

Choose a clear day, but not a hot one, for this perambulation around the Prime Minister's weekend retreat and prepare yourself for some magnificent views. To achieve these you set off up a very steep hill leading to a memorial to the men of Buckinghamshire who fell in the Boer War. The route follows the Ridgeway across the grounds

Distance: *4¹/₂ miles*

OS Explorer 181 Chiltern Hills North
GR 843070

A very steep start, but then a gentle bridleway through woods and walking along roads

Starting point: The car park by the playground and village hall in Butlers Cross.

How to get there: Butlers Cross is just east of Ellesborough, which itself is 2 miles north-east of Princes Risborough off the A4010.

The Walk

❶ From the car park turn right and right again up Wendover Road, taking extra care when the pavement runs out. As you come alongside the golf course and just before the club house, cross the road and continue straight ahead up the footpath, heading south past the house called Tallboys. Be sure to take the path to the left as there is a choice of three. Continue up the deeply channelled path amongst trees until you reach a white house, where there is an alternative path heading right through a metal gate. This leads to another intersection of paths where you head uphill to the left. The path now becomes very steep, eventually coming out

onto an open space. A final push brings you to the summit of Coombe Hill, marked by a monument to the men of Bucks who fell in the Boer War. The views from here on a clear day are spectacular, with a useful plinth indicating what you are looking at. The monument is in fact a reconstruction as the original, built in 1904, was destroyed by lightning in 1938, which is hardly surprising given its position.

❷ When you have seen your fill continue along the path along the ridge, still heading due south. Chequers is now clearly visible to the right, as is part of the golf course where Tony Blair and Bill Clinton once famously played a round.

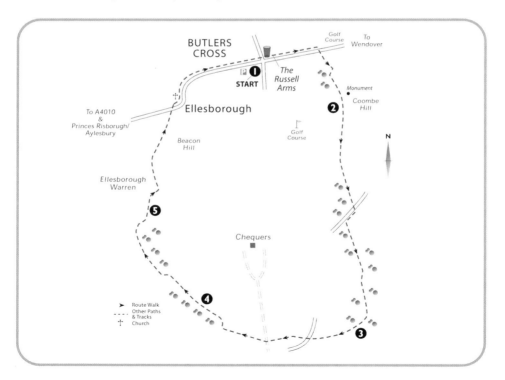

On approaching some trees the path heads left then right through a metal kissing gate and is clearly marked as the Ridgeway. Follow this through some trees until you reach a road where you turn right, heading downhill for 100 yards until you pick up signs for the Ridgeway once again near a metal gate. Re-enter the woods via a stile on your right and keep going straight ahead, ignoring various paths cutting in front of you, keeping an ear open all the time for woodpeckers.

Chequers with the monument on Coombe Hill in the distance

❸ Stick with the Ridgeway as it does another couple of left/right dog-legs before heading downhill to the right, down a steep path, taking the walkers-only option halfway down. On reaching the road cross straight over and follow the path left past a security camera. Keep strictly to the path as it crosses the driveway up to the prime ministerial residence past another camera and straight ahead through two more metal kissing gates. The path now heads uphill across an open field, making for some woods.

❹ On reaching the woods, skirt down the trees to the right following a recently erected fence apparently made of railway tracks – enough to construct a branch line! There are good views here of Chequers and the Boer War monument behind it, which now seems a long way away. On reaching another gate leave the Ridgeway, instead keeping to the right by the woods, following these round to a stile where the path cuts across a back road into the house.

❺ On emerging from the trees strike out across open land with some more excellent views to the left. The path soon descends into a curious geological feature known as Ellesborough Warren and then up and round the side of Beacon Hill. The spire of Ellesborough church is your next target, sitting proudly on its own mound, and is reached by cutting across more fields. On reaching the road in front of the church turn right and pick up the path on the opposite side after 50 yards. After about $1/2$ mile this brings you back to your starting point.

Place of Interest

3 miles south of Butlers Cross you will find the **Home of Rest for Horses** in Speen. It is over 120 years old, the founder was inspired by the book *Black Beauty* and the harsh treatment formerly given to London's horses. Until recently it was the home of Sefton, the horse injured in the Hyde Park bombings. Admission is free and the Home is open from 2 pm to 4 pm except Christmas Day and the day of their AGM. Telephone: 01494 488464.

Date walk completed:

....

Pop stars, maharishis, prime ministers and grand larceny all star in this gentle stroll around the edge of Mentmore Park. The walk starts in the charming village of Mentmore and cuts across to the line of track used by the 1963 Great Train Robbers before dipping into woodland and following the edge of a golf course where the famous Mentmore Towers dominates the scene. The paths are largely flat, except for one section at the end, and are easy to follow, offering a number of spectacular views along the way.

In recent years the **Stag** has earned something of a reputation for its food. Both bar and restaurant meals are available, with the former including a varied and interesting selection of lunches – exotic sandwiches, unusual salads and spicy local sausages. Local is the watchword in the restaurant too, with even the mozzarella cheese coming from a nearby buffalo herd. The accent is on good British food, which can be eaten inside or in the extensive gardens. The pub includes a cosy public bar serving Charles Wells beers as well as guest ales.

Opening times are 12 noon to 3 pm and 6 pm to 11 pm on Monday to Friday and all day at weekends. Food is served from 12 noon to 2 pm and 7 pm to 9 pm (7 pm to 8.30 pm on Sunday), although the restaurant is closed on Monday and there is no bar food on Monday evenings.

Telephone: 01296 618423.

Distance: 6 miles

OS Explorer 181 Chiltern Hills North and 192 Buckingham and Milton Keynes GR 908197

Mostly flat using bridleway and minor roads, with one steep hill near the end

Starting point: Roadside parking near the Stag in Mentmore.

How to get there: Mentmore is 5 miles north-east of Aylesbury off the A418 towards Leighton Buzzard.

The Walk

1 Turn left from the pub, heading downhill, following the road as it bends. Just after it straightens take the footpath to the left over a stile and into a cultivated field. Follow the edge of the field until a marker sends you over it towards some houses, aiming to their left. On reaching them, continue in a south-easterly direction, keeping the large hedge to your left, but first pause to look behind you at the view of Mentmore Towers rising up on the hill. The house has an interesting history. Originally built for the Rothschild family in the mid-19th century it became the property of Lord Rosebery, one-time prime minister, and in more recent times was bought by George Harrison as the headquarters of the Natural Law Party.

2 Continue along this clearly defined track even when the hedge gives out, staying under the telephone wire that bisects the large field. The railway line you can see is just south of the spot where the Great Train Robbery took place in 1963, selected because it was isolated, had a signal and was easy to access by road.

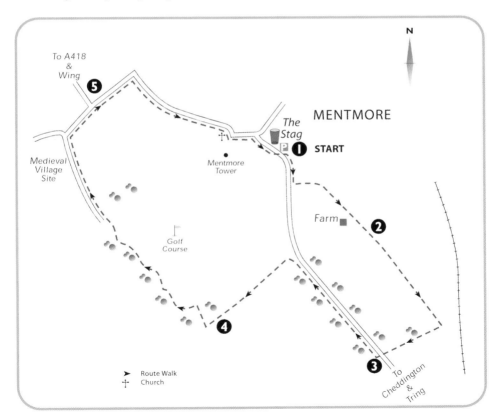

On reaching an elegant house with a dovecot near the railway station turn right, and keep on this path where it is signed as a public bridleway heading for Mentmore – a pleasant amble sandwiched between a hedge on one side and a beech and fir plantation on the other.

3 When the plantation peters out cross the road and pick up the path on the other side over a small wooden platform above a ditch. Head right towards Mentmore and its sandy-coloured towers up ahead, walking amongst a line of trees, making sure to stick to the left of the ditch, which is all too easy to fall into. Pass the entrance to the golf club and pick up the path on the left as it nears the picturesque thatched gatehouse. Walk along the road by the side of the golf course, heading for the woods.

4 Around 100 yards past the greenkeeper's stores the path turns into these woods and then traces their edge along the golf course boundary, meandering like an elderly river along a thin line of trees known as 'The Belt'. On approaching the north-west corner of the course the path heads left through a gate and then right along a minor road. Continue on this until you reach a T-junction where you turn right, but pause to look in the bumpy field on your left before doing so as this is the site of a medieval village.

5 When joined by a more significant road continue straight ahead, following signs for Mentmore, taking care at the next two bends both of which are blind and sharp and traffic has a habit of speeding up here. By this point the tops of your thighs may have alerted you to the

Mentmore Towers was once owned by Beatle, George Harrison

fact that you've been walking up a slight gradient for some while and as you round the next bend you will need to gird yourself for a final steep hill ahead, on top of which sits the church of St Mary the Virgin. The final stretch of road brings you back into the village and your starting point, offering splendid views over the flatlands of Bedfordshire on the way, as well as the imposing blue gates at the entrance to Mentmore Towers.

Place of Interest

Like Mentmore Towers, **Ascott House,** south of the A418 near Wing, was a Rothschild house and was extended extensively from its Jacobean origins during their ownership. The house now contains an exceptional painting collection as well as Oriental porcelain and English and French furniture and also has a formal garden. Opening times vary so it is best to phone ahead. Telephone: 01296 688242.

Date walk completed:

The Boot

The towpath belongs to the Aylesbury Arm of the Grand Union Canal, with the walk covering nearly half of this waterway and following it up to its junction with the main canal.

Much of the Boot was recently converted from a restaurant to a shop, making it a highly flexible village resource offering not only food and drink but services that range from newspapers and groceries to dry cleaning and photocopying. The pub itself is a free house with a range of real ales and lagers. The hard-working landlord offers a select menu of staple pub food including pies, jackets and sandwiches, as well as an extensive mixed grill, fish and chips, fisherman's pie and the occasional exotic alternative.

Opening times: Given the dual purpose of the pub it is open most of the time during the day for snacks and coffees, although alcohol and food are served within licensing hours at the landlord's discretion.

Telephone: 01296 668359.

T hrough an easy combination of roads, fields and towpath this walk explores the area contained within an odd spur of the Hertfordshire border that stabs into heart of Buckinghamshire.

Distance: *6¹/₄ miles*

OS Explorer 181 Chiltern Hills North
GR 895158

A level and relatively easy walk

Starting point: Outside the Boot by the war memorial.

How to get there: Long Marston is 3 miles north-west of Tring and is best reached via Marsworth, which lies on the B489 between Ivinghoe and Aston Clinton.

The Walk

❶ Head down Chapel Lane, opposite the Boot and adjacent to the war memorial. Pass Church Farm and the recently restored church tower of Long Marston, all that is left of the original church that was demolished due to instability. The road opens up and the footpath heads half-left over a pair of stiles and along the edge of a field. Cross another stile and a plank bridge and continue forward, keeping the field boundaries to your left. At the end of the second field go through a metal gate and head for Puttenham church tower in front of you, passing over the pair of wooden bridges to your left and then right just before the church.

It is worth pausing to look at the church, which dates back to the 14th century and is of an interesting flint and stone checkerboard construction.

❷ Take the road to the left past Manor Farm and at the junction with another road turn right. At the bend go down the No Through Road. By a modern cottage cross the stile over the road in the corner and then go along the left of the field. Follow the boundary round this and the next field, crossing over the stile in the corner of the second. Go over the track in front of you and then immediately right down an alleyway, which leads, via a pair of stiles, to a more made up track on your left. Join this and go over the canal bridge,

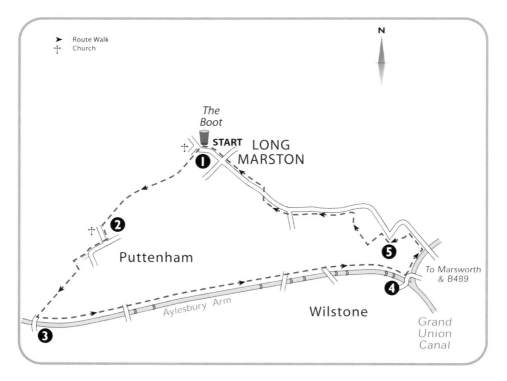

dropping down to the towpath on your left.

3 This is the Aylesbury Arm of the Grand Union Canal and you now head east towards its junction with the main canal. This stretch is almost Roman in its straightness, although the journey is enlivened by a series of locks. By one of these there is a yard using traditional methods to repair narrowboats and by lock 5 there is an unusual seat made out of an old lock balance beam. Continue past the outskirts of Wilstone (where the last recorded witch hunt in England took place in 1751) and on to locks 1 and 2 at the junction. These comprise the only staircase lock on the southern part of the Grand Union – a challenging introduction to the Aylesbury Arm for those coming the other way.

4 Cross over the lock carefully and follow the Grand Union round to the left, past the British Waterways offices. Head north to the second bridge you come to, distinguished by the sign advertising the Red Lion in Marsworth. Leave the canal here by turning left onto a road, using the pavement on the right. Just before a garage there is a footpath on the other side of the road. Take this and pass through the kissing gate in the corner of the field and then through another at the end of the next field. This leads you back to the road, but cuts out a dog-leg within it.

5 Go straight ahead on the pavement on the right of the road for 50 yards until you reach a further footpath on the other side of the road. Take this and follow the metalled track to its end, crossing into the next field and then immediately turning

The 14th-century flint and stone church at Puttenham

right through a gap in the hedge. Follow this field round its right-hand boundary and on reaching a kissing gate go through and join a signed right of way round to the left. This criss-crosses a stream and passes over the bottom of the garden of a private house until you rejoin the road. Turn left and at the junction a bit further on bear right, following signs to Long Marston. There is no pavement here for 200 yards so take care. Pass the Queen's Head and continue forward until you rejoin the Boot.

Place of Interest
The Walter Rothschild Zoological Museum, in the heart of Tring, houses an extensive and remarkable collection of stuffed birds, insects, fish and animals, including a model of the now extinct dodo. There is a Discovery Room and café and entrance is free. The museum is open from 10 am to 5 pm on Monday to Saturday and 2 pm to 5 pm on Sunday. Telephone: 020 7942 6171.

Date walk completed:

....

The Boot

farm on this picturesque chalk stream and offering plenty of bird-spotting opportunities. The walk starts in Sarratt, which is dominated by a long village green, pockmarked with former ponds, and is where John Le Carré placed his fictional spy school. Along the way there's the 12th-century church of the Holy Cross in Church End and a delightful former granary on the Chess in Chenies.

The **Boot** is an unspoilt village pub facing Sarratt's long village green, with century-old lime trees and modern picnic sets in a large paddock-style garden. The Parlour Bar has an 18th-century inglenook fireplace and a quarry-tiled floor, which complement the low beams and nicely-aged ceiling, as well as various nooks and crannies suitable for spies and lovers alike. The chef has a passion for decent, honest food and offers fresh fish and game in the evening from Wednesday to Saturday, as well as more basic 'Boot Busters' for lunch – filled French bread designed to satisfy the hungriest walker!

A hilly walk up and down the sides of, as well as along, the Chess valley, taking in the last watercress

Distance: 6 miles

OS Explorer 172 Chiltern Hills East GR 043994

Well-defined paths with some challenging hills

Starting point: The Green, Sarratt. Plenty of on-street parking.

How to get there: Sarratt is 2 miles north of Rickmansworth on a minor road off the A404.

Opening times are 12 noon to 3 pm and 5 pm to 11 pm on Monday to Friday; 12 noon to 11 pm on Saturday; 12 noon to 6 pm on Sunday. Food is served 12 noon to 2.30 pm Monday to Saturday and 12 noon to 4 pm on Sunday.

Telephone: 01923 262247.

The Walk

1 Pick up the path signed 'Church End' just south of the post office and follow it over some stepping stones and across a series of pastures which can get quite muddy. Continue down the edge of some woods until you reach an intersection of paths, where you take the one leading half-left over a cow field, marked as the Chiltern Way. Head for the church in the top right-hand corner, but do not cross the stile there, instead doubling back on yourself, keeping the holly hedge to your left until it runs out by a metal gate.

2 Turn left on the other side of the gate down a steep hill. The bed of the Chess valley is now clearly visible and is soon reached via a stile in the bottom left-hand corner of the field and a stepped path through trees. The gentle babbling of the chalk stream is now audible and can be spotted through gaps in the hedge as the path continues to the right along a road. Continue straight ahead at the junction and as the road bends to the right the path heads left down a concrete track, clearly marked as a footpath. This takes you down to the cultivated watercress beds, with the crop thriving in the fast flowing

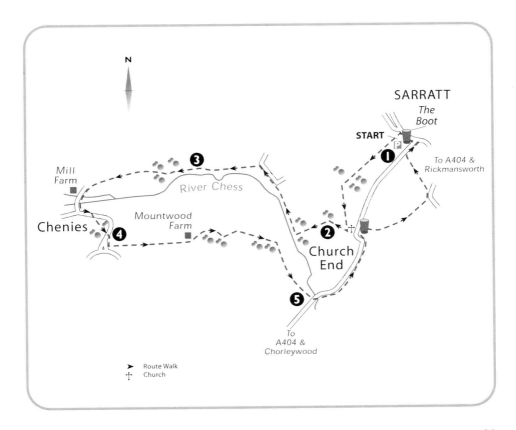

N

SARRATT

The Boot

START

To A404 & Rickmansworth

Mill Farm

3

River Chess

Chenies

4

Mountwood Farm

2

Church End

5

To A404 & Chorleywood

➤ Route Walk
✝ Church

and warm water. The river used to have many such 'farms', but alas, this is the last.

3 Resist the temptation to cross the river, using instead the boardwalk to the right, keeping parallel to the water. Path and river diverge for a while, but stay on the well-defined and trodden path through some trees, keeping to the valley floor. At Mill Farm take a left where you can cross the river in two places, sparing time to take in the former granary where cress grows wild in the water before it falls into the mill race below. Follow the road round to the left where it meets another, more major, road and continue left until you reach an elevated path on the other side. Take this and follow it round and up a steep path.

4 A little road walking is required where the path ends, but you pick up the path again to the left of the triangle of grass, going down a metalled road through some white gates, eventually passing to the right of Mountwood Farm. Ignore the path to the left and skirt the edge of some woods before a hedge where you head diagonally right downhill to the corner of the field. The church at Church End is now clearly visible on the other side of the valley. Cross the stile and pick up the path marked 'Sarratt Mill', heading right along the south bank of the river – a wonderful bird-spotting location.

5 On reaching the road turn left and cross the river again before heading steeply uphill to Church End, where you finally have the chance to visit the 12th-century Holy Cross church with its eclectic collection of tombstones. Follow the road round a dog-leg and pick up the

The clear waters of the River Chess

path on the right by the Cock Inn, where bodies used to be prepared before burial in the churchyard opposite. Cut diagonally left across the field at the fork and cross the stile, keeping the hedge to your left. On reaching the road take the path to your left, heading half-right across a final stretch of field, where a stile in the top corner takes you onto a road. Turn right at the T-junction and left at the flint cottage, past the Cricketers pub and back to your starting point.

Place of Interest

Chenies Manor in Chenies, south-west of Sarratt, is a 15th-century Tudor brick house owned in the past by both the Russells and the Dukes of Bedford. The house is impressive for its massive chimney stacks and the garden for its display of tulips in the spring. Opening hours are limited, so a call ahead is advisable. Telephone: 01494 762888.

Date walk completed:

....

The Walk

1 Pick up the road at the back of the pub and head into Harpenden, past the British Legion and the Inn on the Green until you reach a turning to the left signed to the Sports Centre. Head up this road (where there is some alternative parking) and continue uphill past the tennis club until you reach a bend to the right. At the crown of this bend take the footpath ahead of you, which is signed to Rothamsted and the Nicky Line and comes out onto open ground and a cricket pitch. Follow the back of the houses to your right along the line of high hedges. Skirt the boundary of a

second cricket pitch and in the corner of the playing field take the kissing gate into one of Rothamsted's experimental fields.

2 After a short distance the footpath turns right down a track, bordered initially by high hedges but emerging after a while into open land with a hedge down the left. Follow this hedge, through which it's possible to catch the occasional glimpse of the Research Establishment, until you reach a more major track where you turn left and then almost immediately right, following the left-hand boundary of another field towards some woods.

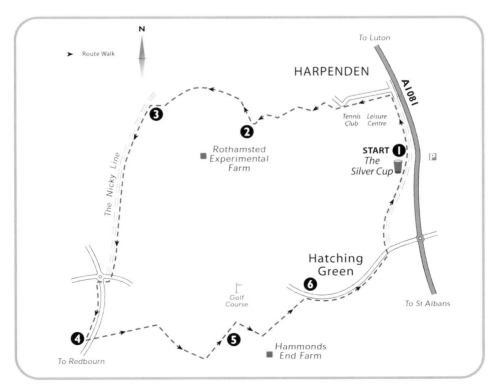

3 On reaching the woods, where there is a wooden seat, turn left at the intersection of paths, following signs for the Nicky Line. This long straight stretch under trees offers shade in the summer but can become slippery in places in the winter. This path is a remnant of an old branch line of the Birmingham Railway, which ran from Harpenden to Hemel Hempstead to link the straw plait industry with the Luton hat trade. Continue downhill straight ahead, ignoring an intersection of paths, until you reach a road. Cross this and turn right, crossing the next road heading towards St Albans, and picking up the Nicky Line again, signed here as route 57 on the National Cycle Network.

4 On reaching a concrete road turn left and cross the road once again, going up a steep flight of wooden steps and over a stile into a field. The footpath cuts half-left over this field, following the line of some telegraph poles. This heads uphill but offers some good views. At the top of the field enter another and keep to the right-hand side. Bear right then left at the next set of paths, which takes you into some trees. Follow this path along until you emerge unexpectedly onto a golf course. Turn right and then left in the corner by the 8th tee, where a water fountain has thoughtfully been provided.

5 Keep to the right down the side of the golf course and pick up the path on the right just before it reaches a road. This takes you into some more trees and past the Georgian magnificence of Hammonds End Farm, which stands imperiously on its own over to your right. On emerging back onto the course, the path heads left over the grass (so watch out for golf balls)

Walkers and cyclists use the Nicky Line these days

and eventually comes out on a small road where you turn left.

6 On reaching Redbourn Lane turn right and follow the pavement downhill to, and then through, Hatching Green, going past a number of very impressive houses. Just before the main road pick the path up again on the left, where it resumes the form of a back road. Continue along here past rows of cottages, including a thatched one, and the imposing entrance to Rothamsted Park until you come back to the Silver Cup.

Place of Interest

Redbournbury Mill, 2 miles north of St Albans on the A5183, dates back to the 15th century and was recently restored to working order. Now the only working mill on the River Ver, it is open on Sunday afternoons during the summer and other selected days. Telephone: 01582 792874.

Date walk completed:

Ye Olde Fighting Cocks

short stretch across fields and along a country lane to allow a sweep round the park and the opportunity to take in a vista which encompasses all of the town, ancient and modern.

The site of **Ye Olde Fighting Cocks** has records going back to AD 793, although the main part of the structure today is an octagonal room dating from around 1600. Inside the floor drops down into a pit, once used for the unsavoury sport from which the pub gains its name. Oliver Cromwell is reputed to have stabled his horse one night in the pub, but it is unlikely that he enjoyed anything like the gastronomic range offered today, with the menu ranging from steak pie to leek and gruyère parcels, as well as a full range of sandwiches, jacket potatoes and salads. The pub is family friendly and its beer garden is frequented by locals and tourists alike in the summer.

St Albans positively oozes history, and this short and relatively easy walk gives plenty of scope to sample some of it. Its central feature is the site of the Roman town of Verulamium, but it also offers grand views of the dominating cathedral dedicated to St Alban, the country's first Christian martyr. Much of the walk is paved, although there is a

Distance: *3¹/₂ miles*

OS Explorer 182 St Albans and Hatfield GR 138075

Largely paved and lawn with some gentle inclines

Starting point: Verulamium Museum car park.

How to get there: The museum lies off the A4147 on the west side of St Albans, near the junction with the A5183, and is well signposted.

Opening times are 12 noon to 11 pm every day (Sunday to 10.30 pm). Food is served from 12 noon to 2.30 pm and 6 pm to 8 pm on Monday to Friday and from 12 noon to 5 pm on Saturday and Sunday.

Telephone: 01727 869152.

The Walk

❶ Walk back to the entrance to the car park and down pretty St Michael's Street. Just before the bridge near Kingsbury Mill turn right into Verulamium Park. Follow the path with the River Ver to your left and the artificial lake to your right. This lake was created as part of a work scheme in the Great Depression but it has longer antecedents, the site marking the spot where fishponds once existed to supply the monks in the abbey. Carry on until you reach the corner of the lake where you will find the Fighting Cocks pub. The route requires you to turn right, taking the paved raised path. At this point you begin to leave the river, and soon the lake too, behind you.

❷ The route channels a path between a deep ditch to your left and a long stretch of ruins of the wall that once bounded the Roman town to your right. The latter begins with the remains of the wall's London Gate and it is worth pausing here to read the information board. At the top of the hill cross the bridge over the ditch and you come to a modern road. Cross the road using the pedestrian crossing and continue straight ahead along a footpath running alongside some disused playing fields.

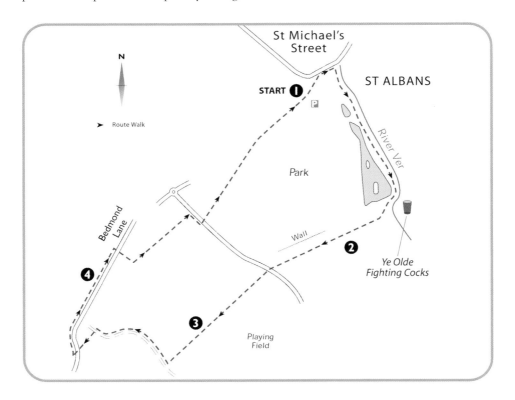

St Michael's
Street

N

ST ALBANS

START ❶

River Ver

Route Walk

Park

Bedmond Lane

Wall

❷

Ye Olde
Fighting Cocks

❹

❸

Playing
Field

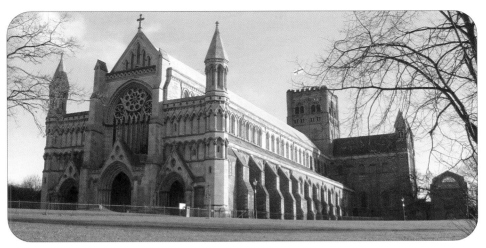

The spectacular St Alban's cathedral

3 Stick with the path, crossing two roads in a modern housing estate. Turn right at the third road and continue along its left-hand edge, passing a triangle of grass on your right. Carry on into Mayne Avenue, following the road down first to the left and then to the right, picking up a footpath on the bend in the road (marked as number 32A). Cut across the corner of the following field and then bear right onto Bedmond Lane.

4 Follow the lane round, going slightly uphill until you reach another footpath on the right, keeping an eye out for traffic as you do so. Take this path and bear left just before it reaches the residential road, following it round the back of some houses until you come to a busy main road. Cross this using the pedestrian crossing 50 yards to your right and go straight on back into Verulamium Park, taking in the spectacular views of the cathedral ahead of you. It was on this site that Boudicca famously rose up against the Romans and centuries later Wat Tyler led a very different kind of peasants' revolt. These days any shouting is likely to be confined to the football pitches you pass as you head across the grass and downhill. Soon the impressive portico of Verulamium Museum comes into view in front of you, preceded by the car park and the point where you started the walk.

Places of Interest

Verulamium Museum, near the car park, specialises in displaying everyday life in a Roman town and has a number of re-created rooms and hands-on discovery areas. Telephone: 01727 751810.

Also take time to view the **Abbey**, which houses the shrine to St Alban. Telephone: 01727 860780.

Date walk completed:

Bedfordshire border. There are good views across rolling hills and even a converted windmill towards the end. The walk also serves as a reminder of what might be lost should the airport be allowed to expand further, with the delicate balance between nature's bounty and human needs amply demonstrated.

It's difficult to believe when doing this walk that you're on the edge of a busy industrial town and an even busier international airport. Passing through two quiet villages the walk utilises both country lanes and footpaths to guide you through the rural hinterland at the Hertfordshire/

Distance: 3³/₄ miles

OS Explorer 193 Luton and Stevenage
GR 137232

A combination of country lanes and field footpaths with some hills

Starting point: The centre of Tea Green (park in pub car park with the landlord's permission).

How to get there: Tea Green is 3 miles north-east off the A505. Take the turning just north of Luton Airport to the south of Luton.

The **White Horse** is the focal point of this small village. It has a large car park and a garden with children's play equipment. The bar has an unusual slated wooden front and there's a side room for quiet dining. The menu is extensive and aimed at families, covering sections devoted to 'Lite Bites', steaks and grills, vegetarian, fish and curries. The Lite Bites include a choice of four mixed platters whilst the vegetarian section lists dishes such as Mediterranean lasagne and harvester pie. There are daily specials, with such fare as West Country pork chop or pepperoni chicken.

Opening times are 11 am to 3 pm and 5.30 pm to 11 pm on Monday to Saturday; 12 noon to 10.30 pm on Sunday. Food is served from 12 noon to 2.30 pm and 6 pm to 9.30 pm on Monday to Saturday and 12 noon to 9 pm on Sunday.

Telephone: 01582 722855.

The Walk

1 In Tea Green head south, down the left-hand edge of the grass triangle as you leave the pub car park, signposted to Wandon End. On reaching another grass triangle head right, still signed to Wandon End and also to Luton, going past a farm on your right and staying on the lane rather than taking the footpath on your right. Continue along the lane past a golf driving range and up ahead you may make out the tails of planes gathered on the edge of Luton Airport.

2 Turn left at the junction by Wandon End Farm and continue along this new lane with the airport now on your right.

This now heads downhill along a series of bends. Keep straight ahead at the first junction and keep to the left at a second junction, picking up a path on the right shortly afterwards. This is signed as the Chiltern Way and is also a public bridleway. Head off over the open fields in front of you. The path is clearly defined but can get a bit overgrown in places, but it's impossible to go wrong if you aim for the small clump of trees in front of you.

3 On reaching these trees pass through them and pick up the path on the left-hand boundary of a new field alongside a fence. On reaching a junction of paths maintain your direction by going straight ahead – the path now loses its bridleway

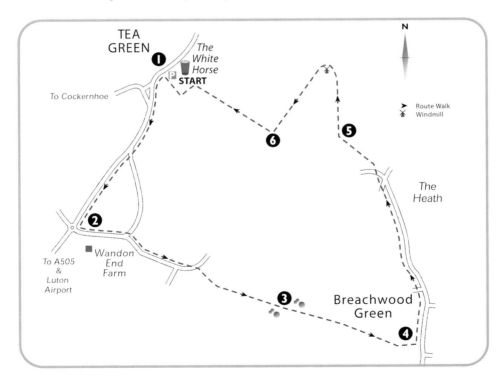

103

status and becomes a simple footpath. The path turns right along the edge of a field and then almost immediately left across the field. On reaching a fence bear right, initially following the edge of a field before twisting and turning along a series of bends. These end at a kissing gate, which in turn brings you out onto a road where you turn left.

4 Follow the road into the small village of Breachwood Green and take care to notice both the tan coloured half-timbered house on the left and the ornate Baptist chapel on the right as you go. There's also another pub here, the Red Lion (tel. 01438 833123). Continue all the way through the village and an area known as The Heath with its row of attractive flint cottages, which are richly bedecked with hanging baskets of flowers in the summer. Maintain your direction at the crossroads and when the road bends you should also continue forward down Windmill Road.

5 Bear right along the lane when the houses run out, following the track to the black sail-less structure from which the road gets its name. The windmill has been converted into a private residence and is not open to the public, although you can admire it from outside. Pick up the path along the field in front of the windmill, taking the spur on the left after around 30 yards, cutting across the field. As you crest a short hill the outskirts of the airport become visible again and you are reminded how close you are to this major transport hub, which has been easy to forget. The path comes out onto a T-junction where you turn right and then immediately left to maintain your south-westerly direction.

The rolling hills around Tea Green

6 On reaching another T-junction turn right again but this time keep going, now heading in a north-westerly direction towards a white concrete water tower. On reaching yet another T-junction bear left, ignoring the path on your right shortly afterwards. This bends to the right and cuts across the end of a field to come out on a patch of grass and the back of the car park of the White Horse. Either pop into the pub or walk through to re-acquaint yourself with the centre of Tea Green.

Place of Interest

Stockwood Craft Museum and Gardens, on the southern edge of Luton (reached from Tea Green via the A505 and the A1081), is a free museum displaying Bedfordshire rural life including a craft section, a bee gallery and a sculpture garden. It is open all year round and also stages special events. Telephone: 01582 738714.

Date walk completed:

....

The Brocket Arms

perhaps The Flood'. The walk begins and ends with stretches of footpaths threading through fields, with woodland and a river providing contrast, and a stroll along a quiet country lane in the middle. Having started at the Brocket Arms, it is appropriate that the walk's destination is 18th-century Brocket Hall, where Henry VIII wooed Catherine Parr.

The three Ayot villages of north Hertfordshire present an idyllic image of England. Sir George Bernard Shaw lived and wrote in Ayot St Lawrence, the starting point of this walk, and said of it 'the last real thing of importance that happened to it was

Perhaps inappropriately, the 14th-century **Brocket Arms** was originally the monastic quarters for the local Norman church. These days it has a beautifully maintained walled garden outside and an inglenook fireplace inside, with ancient oak beams dominating the small bar and restaurant, both of which have plenty of character. Bar snacks are available at lunch and dinner, with à la carte candlelit restaurant meals served in the evening. The speciality here is game, but there are also home-cooked traditional dishes such as lamb cutlet with redcurrant sauce and steak and kidney pie, although you may also find fish such as pan-fried sea bass on the menu.

Distance: 6$\frac{1}{2}$ miles

OS Explorer 182 St Albans and Hatfield GR 197168

A combination of country lanes and bridleways with two fairly steep inclines

Starting point: Park on the road outside the Brocket Arms, which is to the north of the village.

How to get there: Ayot St Lawrence is a mile to the east of the B651 between Wheathampstead and Kimpton north of St Albans.

Opening times are 11 am to 11 pm (10.30 pm on Sunday). Food is served from 12 noon to 2.30 pm and 7.30 pm to 9.30 pm on Tuesday to Saturday; and on Sunday from 12 noon to 2.30 pm.

Telephone: 01438 820250.

The Walk

1 Turn left out of the pub and follow the road round past the ruins of the old church of Ayot St Lawrence and at the bend pass down the path in front of you briefly to see the white façade of Ayot House on the right, once famous as Britain's only silk farm. Retrace your steps and turn right, heading downhill towards Shaw's Corner, which is signposted and can't be missed due to its name being etched into its main gate. Go past the entrance to Shaw's old home and continue with the road as it bends left until there is a short straight stretch. At the end of this there's a footpath to the

right of a house called 'Amesbury', which is signposted to Codicote Road. A bridleway, this runs between two hedges and then some trees before opening out to reveal a view to the right over fields and woodlands.

2 After ³/₄ mile the path descends onto Codicote Road and you need to pick the path up again directly opposite with the sign now sending you to Hunter's Bridge. You will not go this far though as on entering the second field you need to turn sharp right towards Threegroves Wood, which you skirt to the left on reaching, before striking off over open land towards another small wood. Pick up the track to

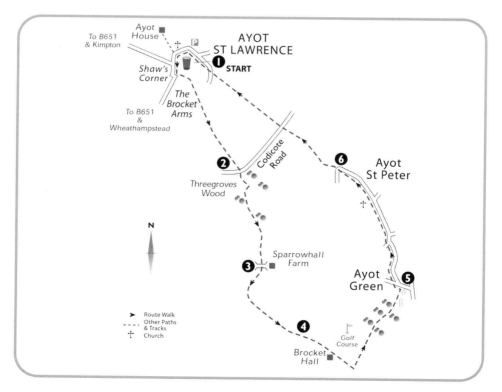

the right of the trees and stick with it as it descends all the way to Sparrowhall Farm, where there is another good view.

❸ Cross over a bridge and on reaching the opening by a barn continue straight over. Walk downhill along the left-hand side of the field and along its top until you reach a corner and a path in front of you that leads to some steps going downhill towards the valley of the River Lea. At the bottom of the steps turn left and then right onto a road by an impressive Tudor house. Head right downhill towards the river but just before reaching it pick up the path on the left signposted to Brocket Hall and walk along the valley floor.

❹ Continue through trees that obscure views of the river itself until you reach an opening. Here you need to walk straight ahead up a short but steep path into the woods, following signs for the Lea Valley Walk. This path twists and turns a bit but eventually emerges onto a golf course where you have to take special care to keep your eyes and ears open as the path crosses over fairways twice! The path now goes past the side of Brocket Hall, sitting in an impressive position beside a lake. Keep going straight on, sticking to the path, past the side of the Hall and up again, picking up the well-signed footpath taking you to the left and into some more trees. Follow this until you reach a road where you turn left to enter the pretty village of Ayot Green.

❺ Turn left into the village proper by the road bridge and take the right-hand fork signposted to Ayot St Peter by the side of the green. Follow this road round for just under a mile, ignoring the road to Homer's Wood, until you reach the

Brocket Hall

church with its unusual war memorial and clockface. Continue with the road until you reach a large white house, Tamarisk Cottage, on a bend.

❻ Take the bridleway on the right and follow this down the middle of two fields until you reach Codicote Road. Continue straight on through three fields before rejoining the road that leads back to the starting point.

Place of Interest

Shaw's Corner, in Ayot St Lawrence, is an Edwardian villa occupied by the famous writer from 1906 until his death in 1950. The rooms have been left in period and the writing hut where Shaw wrote his great works sits at the bottom of the beautiful garden. The house is owned by the National Trust and is open on Wednesday to Sunday from March to October. Telephone: 01438 820307.

Date walk completed:

....

The Red Lion

contrast the woods are mostly mature and wonderfully wild, like the remnant of a long-past landscape, and it's easy to get lost in them, so you might find a compass useful.

The **Red Lion** was the country's first community-owned pub, saved from closure by the local residents who bought it from the brewery in 1983. It is now renowned for its focus on good real ales and has an impressive collection of beer mats pinned around the head of the bar to prove its credentials. Highly varnished wooden furniture and a stone flag floor provide a pleasant ambience for eating, with dishes available varying from sandwiches at lunchtime to home-made lamb pasty or spinach, Stilton and asparagus quiche and roasts every Sunday. The chef also likes to offer fish when available.

Wide bridleways and woods are the main theme of this walk, which also uses some short stretches of country lanes, at one point going past a charming duck pond. The paths cut across and along wide fields, most of which are cultivated, and the effort of climbing a few short hills is rewarded with some good views. By

Opening times are 12 noon to 2.30 pm and 5.30 pm to 11 pm (10.30 pm on Sunday). Lunches are served from 12 noon to 2 pm and evening meals from 7 pm to 9 pm (no food is available Sunday or Monday evenings).

Telephone: 01462 489585.

Distance: *5¹/₂ miles*

OS Explorer 193 Luton and Stevenage GR 181247

Some short sharp hills but otherwise mainly bridleways and country lanes

Starting point: The Red Lion. Park by the green in Preston or in the layby outside the church.

How to get there: Preston lies 2 miles due south of Hitchin, west of the B656.

The Walk

1 Starting at the pub car park, head for the old well mechanism in the corner of the green and turn left down Church Lane. Pass the rather modern-looking church on your right, complete with a red-tiled and rose-covered lychgate. Turn right at the crossroads down Butchers Lane. Head uphill and on reaching Holly Tree House on your right pick up the path on your left through a kissing gate. This is signed as a Chiltern Way Extension and cuts half-right across a field, aiming for Pond Farm.

2 Pass to the left of the farm and veer

further left, aiming for the stile on the top corner. Cross over and turn right, keeping to the right-hand boundary of the resulting field and coming out onto a kissing gate at a junction of paths by a rough track. Pass through this and turn right, heading uphill through trees and high hedges. When the trees clear to the left there's another junction of paths where you turn left and head downhill, following the left-hand edge of a field along a path marked by a sign with red arrows. The path swaps over onto the right-hand edge of the next field and comes out onto a road.

3 Cross over and maintain your

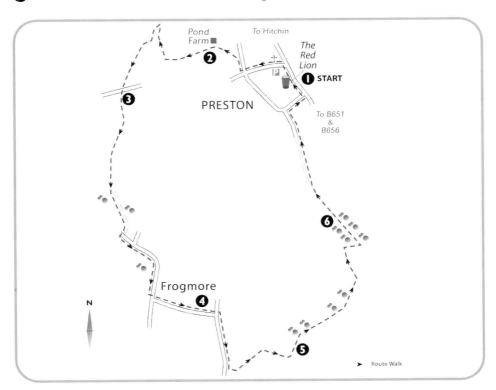

direction, with the path marked as a public byway and retaining its red arrows. This passes steadily downhill through trees and then bottoms out in a clearing before heading uphill, again through trees and hedges. The path starts to be more defined and curves left, after which it becomes a bona fide lane passing a run of houses. On reaching a T-junction turn left and then go right at the next junction by a half-timbered cottage called Whitehall. The road here is signed to Bendish and Whitwell and runs quite steeply downhill. On reaching Frogmore with its pond, turn left at the stables and continue along the lane.

❹ Turn right at Frogmore Bottom and continue a little further until you reach a Goldilocks-style white cottage with yellow shutters on the left. Just after this, turn left down a track. At the bottom of the hill turn left again and bear right at the next fork. As you start to climb don't be surprised to find there's another path above you, the flight path into Luton Airport! On reaching a clearing, head to the top left-hand corner and pick up the path on your left by a dead tree.

❺ This heads steadily uphill into some woods with a wonderfully mature oak at its entrance. Keep straight ahead, ignoring a path to the left, and skirt the right-hand edge of another wood until you come into a field. Follow this along until you reach a red-brick farmhouse where you need to turn left. Follow this path down and head half-right towards some more woods where you turn right. Walk along the left-hand edge of a large field for 300 yards until a path sends you left into the heart of the woods.

One of the lovely views to be enjoyed along the way

❻ Follow the track along, trying to maintain your direction. This stretch is used by riders and can get churned up so take care. The path emerges onto a track where you keep going until it becomes a road, opening onto a grass triangle by a set of three red-tiled cottages where you turn right. On reaching a Georgian house and the entrance to Princess Helena College, turn left and this road brings you back to the pub on your left.

Place of Interest

Waterhall Farm and Craft Centre, on the B651 south of Preston, is an open farm with rare breeds and a number of attractions for children, including a straw bale battlefield, a sand pit and an old tractor, as well as a tearoom and craft centre for the adults. Telephone: 01438 871256.

Date walk completed:

The Cricketers

Large open paths complemented by equally open views make this a walk to savour on a clear day. It starts by following an old bridleway linking the two villages of Weston and Graveley and continues by weaving between fields and roads through a series of woods. Along the way there's an old

Distance: 6¹/₂ miles

OS Explorer 193 Luton and Stevenage
GR 257298

A combination of bridleways and roads makes for easy walking, but with the occasional hill

Starting point: The Cricketers car park (with the landlord's permission) or the small layby opposite.

How to get there: The pub is actually in Damask Green on the edge of Weston which lies just to the east of the B197 below junction 9 of the A1(M) south of Baldock.

disused church and the small hamlet of Warren's Green.

The **Cricketers** has a clean and airy feel with stripped broad floors and green panelling along the walls, and the presence of a small upright piano near the fireplace suggests that when winter comes the locals batten down with a good old singsong. Outside there's a colourful sign depicting cricketers relaxing against the bar, and a large car park with benches. Traditional bar food is served, together with some formal dining, and the emphasis is on fish and steak dishes.

Opening times on Monday to Friday and Sunday are 12 noon to 2.30 pm and 5 pm to 11 pm (10.30 pm on Sunday) and the pub is open all day on Saturday. Food is served 12 noon to 2 pm Tuesday to Sunday and 7 pm to 9 pm Tuesday to Saturday.

Telephone: 01462 790273.

The Walk

1 Turn left out of the car park and take the first road on the left, into a small close of houses at the end of which there is a metal gate leading to a bridleway signposted to Graveley. Enter the field behind the gate and aim for the older of the two gates in the bottom left-hand corner. Pass through this and keep to the left-hand boundary of the following field, reaching a small wooden gate. Go through this and the path passes through the middle of a large cultivated field.

2 Continue in the same direction until you meet a T-junction just before some woods, where you need to turn left towards some trees. On reaching these

be sure not to enter the woods, instead skirting the edge until the end, where you pass through a hedge, keeping the woods to your right. The trees soon peter out, leaving a steady fall downhill towards Graveley, with a succession of excellent views across North Herts along the way. It's difficult to go wrong along this section, just stick to the broad track, which only narrows down when you start the final descent into Graveley.

3 On reaching a gravel driveway continue down towards the church, leaving a barn behind you, where you need to bear left and then left again on reaching the road. Follow the road round until you reach a pretty half-timbered cottage where you turn right. Make sure

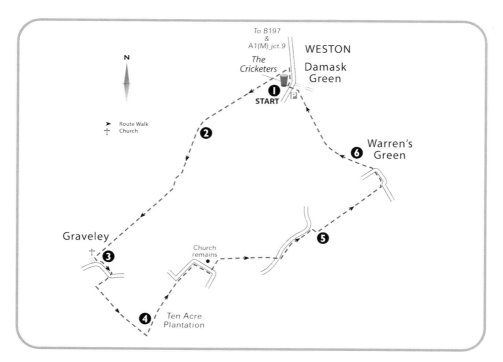

that you pick up the path marked with a circle, which follows the right-hand edge of a pasture. On reaching the next field bear left, keeping the hedge to your left, staying in the same direction when the hedge runs out, where you pass over open ground.

4 On reaching a new hedge bear right and follow the side of what has now become a small copse known locally as the Ten Acre Plantation. On reaching the road turn right. Ignore the footpath signs in front of you at the first sharp bend to the right and take the more minor road at the next bend, which heads left and has a sign leading you to Tusk Carpentry. You will shortly reach the remains of an old church, where you need to follow the sign taking you right. This path passes a small tree nursery and emerges onto a road where you turn left. On reaching Tile Kiln Farm turn right and follow the driveway round, picking up the path on the right by a pond belonging to one of the houses.

5 Cross over a stile and keep to the left through the field, passing through a kissing gate and along the left-hand side of another cultivated, and quite large, field. A metal gate at the end of this brings you back to the road, which you join briefly by turning left, following the bend in the road and ignoring the path tempting you to go straight ahead. Pass Warren's Green Cottages and pick up the path straight in front and a metal kissing gate marked 'The Weston Golden Jubilee Walk'.

6 Another gate follows, after which you pass through some open grazing, edging slightly to the right at the trees. On reaching a third stile and a farm track

The ruins of a church passed on the route

cross over and take the path marked with a circle, leaving the Golden Jubilee Walk which now heads away to the north-east. Follow the path across open land until you reach a road, which, if you turned right, would take you to Weston House and the cricket pitch. However, your route instead requires you to go left and up to a T-junction, where you will see the pub ahead of you to your right.

Place of Interest

Benington Lordship, 4 miles to the east of Stevenage off the A602 or reached from Weston via Cromer and the B1037, is home to a hundred-year-old garden now being looked after by the third generation of the same family. Best seen in spring and autumn, the garden is a mass of colour and sculptures, with formality and wildness combined in equal measure. There's also a Norman keep next to the house. Telephone: 08701 261709.

Date walk completed:

113

The Lytton Arms

reach of both Stevenage and Welwyn, ending up at one of the county's most appreciated pubs. Towards the end there are some good views but this is ideally a walk for spring or autumn when the majesty of the trees can best be enjoyed.

The **Lytton Arms** extends over a number of levels, with a recently added conservatory and patio area having increased its capacity considerably. Designed in 1877 by Sir Edwin Lutyens, brother-in-law to Lord Lytton, the pub seeks to retain an old-fashioned feel with its stripped floor in the main bar and by rejecting modern bar games, relying on its food and focus on real ales (it claims to have served 2,600 different types in the past ten years) to encourage visitors. The menu has something for everyone and ranges from basic bar snacks to delights such as chargrilled lamb's liver and bacon through to luxury steak and kidney pudding. Sausages are also a speciality, and the pub has regular barbecues in the summer.

T his walk starts with a little-known public right of way through part of the Knebworth Country Park, affording a clear view of the house and its surroundings. It continues through deep woodland and along country lanes, providing a pleasant stretch within easy

Opening times are 11 am to 11 pm on Monday to Saturday; 12 noon to 10.30 pm on Sunday. Food is served from 12 noon to 2.30 pm and 7 pm to 9.30 pm (no food on Sunday evenings).

Telephone: 01438 812312.

Distance: *5¹/₂ miles*

OS Explorer 193 Luton and Stevenage and 182 St Albans and Hatfield
GR 228203

Although largely gentle field and roadside walking, there are some gradients and an awkward ladder stile (point 2) which may make this walk unsuitable for some

Starting point: Either the pub car park (with the landlord's permission) or the lane by the green opposite.

How to get there: Old Knebworth lies just south-west of junction 7 of the A1(M).

The Walk

1 Turn right out of the pub towards Old Knebworth. On reaching the triangle of grass bear left and head downhill, following signs to Knebworth Park Cricket Club. Take care here as this short section has no pavement. Just by an old black and white cottage the path begins on the left through an old metal turnstile. This leads you straight into the Country Park and is not well signed, but it is a public footpath, as is verified by the fact that it continues (with a sign) to the right. Pass the cricket ground and head for the church, turning into the churchyard

and bearing left. The path does now have signs, presumably on the basis that once you're in, the estate wants you to go the right way, and sends you out over open lawn with a fine view of Knebworth House to your left. Head for the road that goes behind the house and ends in a car park, but before then the path bears right (again clearly signed) towards a small fenced-off area.

2 Pass to the right of the fenced-off area and aim for the woods in front of you, which mark the northern boundary of the park. As you get nearer this be careful, as although marked on maps as a lake the

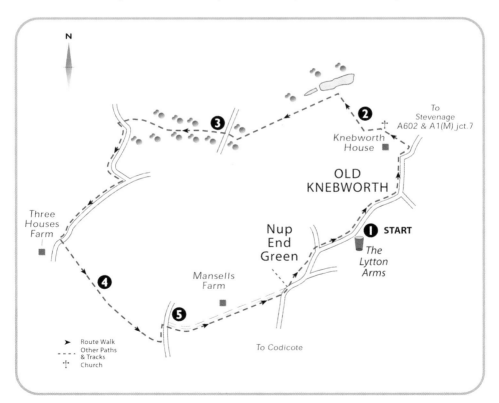

area in front of you is more like a marsh and it's easy to suddenly get your feet wet. You need to turn left here before the reeds and continue along awhile until you reach a fence with a series of footpath markers. Turn right and use the unusual ladder stile to enter some woodland. Cross over a road and pick up the path on the other side.

3 The path here is deeply rutted and runs through a wood, diverting away to the right after a few hundred yards, and after a small clearing it heads left into a beech forest. Follow the clearly marked path through the trees until you reach a minor road, where you head left and downhill. On reaching a junction turn right, following signs to Whitwell. Keep an ear out for cars along this stretch, although there's usually plenty of grass verge to step onto if required. Just before Three Houses Farm the path heads left through a gap in the hedge and follows the left-hand boundary of a field. Keep the regimented pines to your left, although you do need to look out for the potholes at the base of the trees.

4 After the pines the path cuts the corner off a cultivated field and then goes over a stile to cut the corner off another, and finally the left-hand corner off yet another before picking up the field's left-hand boundary for a short while and then striking out across the middle. Keep your head up and eyes open here as there are long views either side. After meeting the boundary again the path emerges onto another road, this one more major and consequently very busy, where you need to go left and uphill for 100 yards until you reach Mansells Lane.

An unusual ladder stile

5 Go along this track past Mansells Farm and on reaching the main road bear left and pick up the second footpath on the left after the house. This leads half-right (north-east) over open ground, with each end marked by a stile. Turn left onto the road at the other end (a pavement soon materialises on the left) and follow this, bearing right at Nup End Green, back to the Lytton Arms.

Place of Interest

It would be a shame not to visit **Knebworth House**. Well known for its rock concerts and various screen roles, Knebworth is a gothic mansion that has been owned by the Lytton family since 1490. Telephone: 01438 812661.

Date walk completed:

....

Little Berkhamsted 37

The Five Horseshoes

Perched above the Lea valley, this walk joins two small villages via a golf course and offers a number of wide-ranging panoramas. Little Berkhamsted, not to be confused with its larger namesake, was the birthplace of Brian Johnston, whilst Beatrix Potter stayed with her grandmother outside Essendon and is known to have loved the area. Added bonuses include a 100 ft high folly-tower sitting proudly on top of the hill and two contrasting churches, both of which are worth a visit.

The part-Tudor **Five Horseshoes** used to be known as the Three Horseshoes, as horses would turn up at the forge that originally stood here minus a shoe, but five was seen as luckier! Inside, the pub is dark and atmospheric, lit by candles and filled with well-used furniture. The walls are lined with row upon row of empty bottles, a prompt to consult the extensive wine list. The menu ranges from the basic to more adventurous dishes such as chicken stuffed with Camembert and wrapped in prosciutto and includes a number of vegetarian options as well as a range of comforting puddings.

Opening times are 11 am to 11 pm every day. Food is served 12.30 pm to 10 pm Monday to Saturday and 12 noon to 9.30 pm on Sunday.

Telephone: 01707 875055.

Distance: *4 miles*

OS Explorer 182 St Albans and Hatfield GR 292077

A gentle undulating walk along firm and easy to follow bridleways and paths

Starting point: Layby opposite the Five Horseshoes or the pub car park (with the owner's permission).

How to get there: Little Berkhamsted is 2 miles south of the A414 east of Hatfield.

The Walk

1 Turn right out of the pub car park past the pretty timber-towered St Andrew's church. The Old Rectory to the east of the church was the birthplace of the cricket commentator Brian 'Johnners' Johnston. Turn right at the war memorial and then left again down Breach Lane, a minor road, following the sign to Howe Green. Look to the left and you will see the top of the circular Stratton Tower, a folly built by Admiral Stratton in the latter half of the 19th century so that he could see shipping on the Thames. These days, this vantage point is better used to admire the views over towards the Lea valley. Just as the road begins to head downhill the path strikes out left across a pasture where the views open out even more until you reach a small concrete footbridge over a stream in the corner.

2 Follow the track between two fields past Ashfield Farm until it becomes a road once more. Follow this along, ignoring the path to your left at a kink in the road, keeping the unmissable chalk and gravel pits to your left. On reaching the houses of Howe Green take the path over a stile just before a white house with a willow at the end of its garden. This leads you

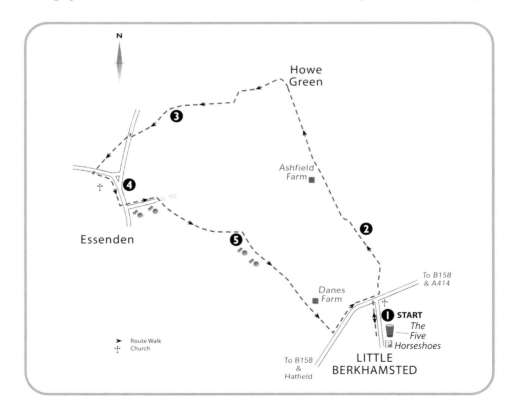

downhill towards a golf course. The spire of Essendon's church is just visible on the horizon and acts as a beacon to aim for. Cross the stile by a stable in the bottom left-hand corner of the field and go left along the road for 50 yards until the path darts into a hedge on the right just before another white house. Look carefully as this is easily missed. This now brings you out onto the golf course via a small bridge over a stream. Follow the path uphill and along a concrete stretch, crossing a number of paths along the way.

There are marvellous views from the top of Stratton Tower

❸ At a T-junction of paths pick up the footpath slightly ahead and to your right, which cuts into some trees, continuing in the same south-westerly direction. This crosses a field and heads for a white wall beside the elegant old Parsonage. On coming onto a road, cross straight over and rejoin the path, which now heads half-left across another pasture, aiming for the end of a run of houses and the church. Cross over the stile and walk left along the road, continuing with it as it curves round to the right, keeping the church of St Mary the Virgin also to your right.

❹ Continue along the High Road for 75 yards until Church Lane, where you head left. Go past the village hall and pick up the path signed as the Hertfordshire Way on your right through some trees, before the school. Keep to the left, ignoring the drive into a house, and this brings you back out onto the golf course, heading downhill towards some attractive landscaping around the club house. Follow the path round the right-hand side of this building and then turn left at the next T-junction, where there is an obscured sign.

❺ This path takes you downhill to Sandpit Lodge where the path continues half-right between some trees, heading uphill, still following the Hertfordshire Way. Continue straight ahead past Danes Farm, where the path's surface is quite solid. On reaching another lodge turn left along the road and follow this until it brings you back to the war memorial, where you turn right and retrace your footsteps back to the pub.

Place of Interest

The magnificent **Hatfield House** lies 2 miles to the west. Built by Robert Cecil in 1611 and given reluctantly to his king, the gardens of this Jacobean house were originally designed by John Tradescant the Elder and are maintained to reflect their former glory. The house and grounds are open from Easter to the end of September, with guided tours of the house on weekdays. Telephone: 01707 287010.

Date walk completed:

....

The Plume of Feathers

explore Tewin, a village of two parts with the Upper half dominated by its cricket green and the Lower by a triangular patch of grass.

Originally one of Queen Elizabeth's hunting lodges, the **Plume of Feathers** later became an inn and then a favoured spot for local highwaymen. These days the light interior in this Greene King house provides a number

This delightful walk combines country lanes with a pleasant stroll alongside the banks of a small stream, ending with a stretch through woods to reach an Elizabethan mansion. There's also the opportunity to

of quiet spots to eat and drink. The garden is a feature, and has a number of games including petanque and even basketball. Spanish tapas are served along with dishes such as red mullet with new potatoes and basil. A speciality is Sunday breakfast and you will need to book for the restaurant.

Distance: 5³/₄ miles

OS Explorer 182 St Albans and Hatfield
GR 272154

Mostly country roads and bridleways with a little field walking; some slight hills

Starting point: The car park at the Plume of Feathers (with the landlord's permission).

How to get there: Tewin lies one mile north of the B1000 just to the east of Welwyn Garden City.

Opening times are 12 noon to 11 pm (closed 3 pm to 6 pm from October to March). Food is served from 12 noon to 2 pm and 7 pm to 9 pm on Monday to Saturday and 12 noon to 2.30 pm on Sunday.

Telephone: 01438 717265.

The Walk

1 Turn right out of the pub car park and follow the footpath sign on the left to reach a pond. Bear left at the pond onto a metalled track and follow this until you reach the Rose and Crown pub. Take the right-hand side of the grass triangle and pick up the footpath on the right (number 17) signed to Digswell. Pass behind an immaculately kept bowling green and then along a track that follows the left-hand edge of a field. On reaching a T-junction with a tall hedge in front of you head left down a public byway to Churchfield Road where you turn left.

2 There is no pavement here, but your passage along the road is short as you take the first right, signed to St Peter's church, by a post box in the wall. On reaching the church, which stands in splendid isolation, pass to the right and turn left heading for the south-east corner of the churchyard. Go through the kissing gate and turn left. Head first down then uphill through some trees and two more kissing gates. Pass a farm on your left and on finding a road turn right and head downhill, ignoring further footpath signs.

3 Follow the road as it bends sharp left and then zig-zags its way down to a

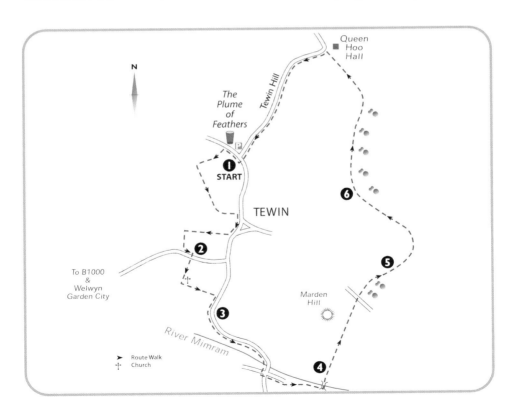

bridge over the beautifully clear River Mimram at the bottom. Cross over this and then another bridge, picking up the footpath on the left just after the second bridge. This is a permissive path through managed water meadows with a variety of grassland and bankside flora, although the entrance can get muddied up by cows so take care. Keep the water to your left and head half-left when the stream runs dry, picking up the first stream. Follow this to a pretty single-spanned stone bridge just before a weir.

The River Mimram at Tewin

4 Cross over the bridge and pass through a kissing gate. Of the two paths take the one on the right heading straight ahead into some trees. The path now becomes a nice wide bridleway and after another kissing gate passes the splendid Georgian pile of Marden Hill. Cross the road and continue on the path in front of you past a large black-tarred barn with its own clockface on your left. On reaching a more significant road pick up the track on the other side, keeping the woods to your right.

5 On sighting the farm on your right keep to the footpath on the left, heading half-left over a field and through a gap in the hedge, maintaining your direction through another, smaller, field to a kissing gate. Head out along the path beyond and pick up the track on the other side, heading left along a series of short curves. On reaching the junction take the left-hand path, heading straight through a field along a track.

6 Continue around the edge of the field at another junction of paths, keeping the high hedge to your right. Stick rigorously to the bridleway all the way to the

Elizabethan hunting lodge Queen Hoo Hall, where you emerge onto a road. Although converted into two labourers' cottages in the 19th century this was restored to its former glory in 1903 and is a perfect example of later Elizabethan brick. You are now at Tewin Hill and you need to turn left and follow it downhill. Just past the farm you will spot the tops of the umbrellas in the Plume of Feathers' garden. On reaching the top of the road turn right back to the pub car park.

Place of Interest
Welwyn Roman Bath House, at the junction of the A1(M) and the A1000, shows the remains of a bath house attached to a Roman villa with a series of 'hot' and 'cold' rooms and a hypocaust. The baths are open from 2 pm to 5 pm at weekends and bank holidays and during school holidays. Telephone: 01707 271362.

Date walk completed:
....

The Jolly Waggoner

Ardeley must have one of the most beautiful village halls and greens in the county, if not the country, and this walk is almost worth doing simply to see them. You should choose this route as well, however, in order to sample a slice of largely forgotten countryside offering good views over flat open fields. There's hardly any sign of human occupation, with only one farm in the middle, giving the opportunity to collect your thoughts before completing the process of unwinding in the Jolly Waggoner, which is the perfect place to satisfy a well-earned appetite.

The 500-year-old **Jolly Waggoner** sits on the main junction in the village and operates as both pub and the Rose Cottage restaurant. The pub is cosy with an oak-beam screen dividing two levels, a lovely tiled floor and walls decorated with highly polished horsebrasses and brass notices. Outside there are benches in a small front garden from which you can watch the world go by. The kitchen offers home-cooked food using local ingredients, with a menu ranging from basic lunches to delights such as wild mushroom and duck pasta or Parma ham roasted and served on stir-fried vegetables. There's also a range of ales and a good selection of wines.

Opening times are 12 noon to 2.30 pm (3 pm on Saturday) and 6.30 pm to 11 pm on Monday to Saturday; 12 noon to 3 pm and 7 pm to 10.30 pm on Sunday. Food is served from 12 noon to 2 pm and 6.30 pm to 9.30 pm on Monday to Saturday; 12 noon to 2 pm on Sunday.

Telephone: 01438 861350.

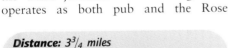

Distance: *3³/₄ miles*

OS Explorer 194 Hertford and Bishops Stortford
GR 308272

Largely flat utilising large byways running mainly through and alongside fields

Starting point: The layby opposite the village hall in Ardeley.

How to get there: Ardeley lies to the south and east of the B1037 linking Stevenage and Buntingford.

The Walk

1 Turn right out of the layby and then immediately right again down Old School Lane. Pass the school on your right and continue until the road peters out and evolves into a track. From this point on for most of the walk the path is what is known as a BOAT, or Byway Open to All Traffic, so you do need to be on your guard against vehicles such as motorbikes or tractors, although you shouldn't encounter too many difficulties. Follow the track around, ignoring invitations to the left and to the right until you meet a clearly marked four-way junction. Here you need to turn left down a hedge-lined path, making sure that it is signed with a red arrow to Wood End.

2 The path is broad and quite firm along here and soon opens up to offer good views over to the north-east towards Buntingford and beyond. At the next junction of paths maintain your direction but at the one after that turn left down a slightly less major path. Walk along the edge of the following field and maintain this direction when the field runs out, following the track round a kink going first left then right as the path passes through some partially wooded and

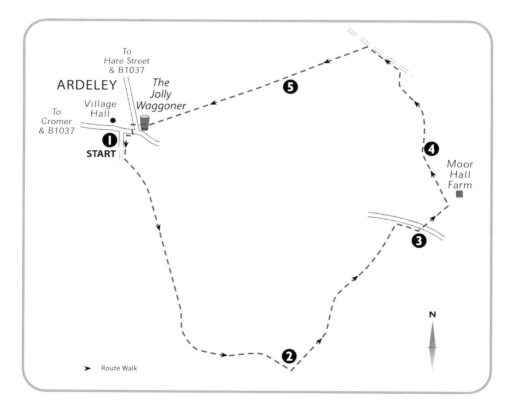

seemingly unused land. The track then emerges into a large open space made up mainly of grass. Pass down the right-hand side of this until you reach a road.

3 Turn right on the road and walk along the edge for less than 100 yards until you pick up a path on the opposite side, still marked with a red arrow. Head up this track to the tar-sided barns of Moor Hall Farm where you need to turn left. The track becomes slightly distressed here and is not well signed, but don't worry as it's only a passing phase and soon there's a stile on the left, which you need to cross in order to pass over a large field heading for some woods.

4 The path leads eventually to a metal gate which you pass through, maintaining your direction once again as you go through another field, this time an uncultivated one, and finally out onto a small country lane. Turn left onto this and follow it round for around 100 yards until you reach a junction with another track where you need to pick up the footpath slightly off the path to the side heading left, signposted to Ardeley. This cuts across a large field, making for some distant trees.

5 Another large field follows, although this time your target is the pencil-thin spire on top of Ardeley's church tower, although as you get closer this gets lost amongst the trees. On reaching the end of the field there's a paddock, which you pass through, turning left on reaching the gravel path and passing some barns. Follow this round to a gap where you will find the Jolly Waggoner behind you on your immediate left. Pause here a while as you wish and pick up the path heading

Take time to admire the green and the village hall at Ardeley

down the road towards the village hall where you will rendezvous with your starting point. Before leaving this walk take time to wander over the road to admire the village hall and the glorious cottages on the other side of the green. There's also what must be an old well mechanism in its own open brick enclosure, complete with weather vane, in the middle of the green. To top off the scene there's also a lily-covered village pond on the other side of the road.

Place of Interest

Cromer Windmill, less than a mile north-west of Ardeley, is the last remaining post mill in Hertfordshire. This magnificent white-wooded construction still has its sails and has been extensively restored. It is open from the second Sunday in May until mid-September on Sundays, bank holidays and the second and fourth Saturday in each month. Telephone: 01279 843301.

Date walk completed:

125

The Old Crown

babbling stream of the River Ash. Contact with the river is direct at a ford visited at both the beginning and end of the circuit. The middle of the walk follows woodland and opens out onto fields on the western edge of the river valley, giving fine views over the local landscape.

The Old Crown announces itself as a family-owned free house, two statements of independence it's easy to believe when you step inside the long thin bar of this popular roadside pub. The owners are justly proud of the pub's Adnams beer and interesting menu, with the latter including delights such as roast duck in plum and cherry sauce or dome of salmon with dill Hollandaise sauce. In fact fresh fish is a speciality from Thursday to Saturday and there are roasts to be had on a Sunday. There's a real fire inside on cold days and a small courtyard outside.

Much Hadham and Hadham Cross are both steeped in history, being once the property of the Bishop of London. This walk offers the opportunity to sample this heritage, including a number of ancient timber-framed houses jutting out into the street, and to enjoy a stroll along the small

Distance: *7 miles*

OS Explorer 194 Hertford and Bishops Stortford
GR 427184

Mostly wood or fieldside walking with some steady slopes either side of the valley

Starting point: Near the post office. Park on the street in Hadham Cross or in the car park opposite the school.

How to get there: Hadham Cross lies on the B1004 to the north-east of Ware, 5 miles north of the A414.

Opening times are 11.30 am to 3 pm and 5.30 pm to 11 pm on Monday to Thursday; 11 am to 11 pm on Friday and Saturday; 12 noon to 10.30 pm on Sunday. Food is served from 12 noon to 2.30 pm and 6.30 pm to 9 pm on Monday to Saturday; 12 noon to 8 pm on Sunday.

Telephone: 01279 842753.

The Walk

1 From the post office head north, leaving the pub behind you, until you reach the flint-faced Old School House where there is a footpath to the right, number 25, signed to Oudle Lane. This slopes gently downhill past the back of some houses to a delightful ford, which can get quite deep in winter. Whatever the season, you're advised to use the raised wooden footbridge and continue along the road on the other side for around 100 yards until you pick up the signed Hertfordshire Way footpath on the left.

2 Aim half-left across the paddock to a

gate and then continue half-left again, aiming for the base of a hill where you are joined by the River Ash. Pass through a pair of gates either side of a drive and continue along the valley floor, crossing over the river itself via a footbridge. Pass through another gate and onto a bend in a metalled road. Take this right and follow it slightly uphill through trees until it bends to the left near a row of pretty white cottages, the last of which is thatched. Follow the bend round to the left (the church should now be on your right), and emerge onto the main road through Much Hadham.

3 Turn left here and pass the half-

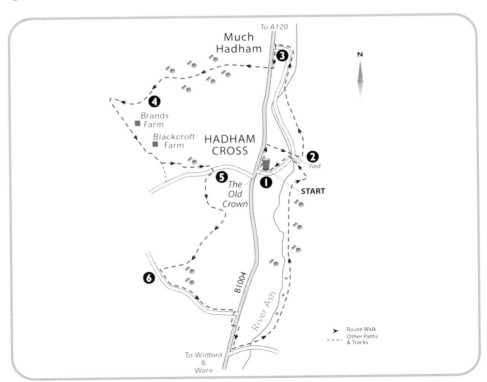

127

timbered rectory. Cross over onto the far side of the road and pick up the path on the right by Tudor Cottage. This leads you onto a public bridleway, which ascends gently but steadily through trees alongside a water channel. Being densely shaded this path doesn't always dry out even in summer and care should be taken in the occasional mud. The path eventually escapes the trees and reaches a track, where you turn left.

4 At the bend in the track take the path straight ahead of you following a marked path with a vivid pink house to your far left. On coming out into an open field take the left-hand option, signed to Kettle Green. This joins a gravel track and takes you past Brands Farm. Just past Blackcroft Farm pick up path number 13 to Hadham Cross on your left. This cuts half-left across a field towards some woods, which it skirts to the right on reaching. On arriving at another track turn left and then right onto a metalled road. Turn right and follow this downhill to a country lane.

5 Turn right and head uphill for 50 yards until you pick up a footpath on your left signed to Windmill Way, which cuts across a large field. On the other side of the field the path goes past the back of some houses and comes out onto a road where you turn right. At the phone box take path number 14 to your right sending you up a No Through Road. Take the right-hand fork at the first house and again at 'Wynches'. The path follows the left-hand boundary of a field and on reaching a road you need to turn left.

6 Head downhill and on reaching the B1004 turn right. Follow this for ⅓ mile

The ford over the River Ash at Hadham Cross

to Bourne Lane where you turn left. After a couple of hundred yards take the bridleway on your left (number 28 to Standsted Hill) through an old council depot. Pick up the Hertfordshire Way in the top left-hand corner, going through a pleasant wooded area where the River Ash rejoins the walk. Continue past the footbridge and through some more woodland until you reach a road where you turn left. Follow this down back to the ford before turning left and following some metal railings to the pub and then your starting point.

Place of Interest
The Forge Museum, on Much Hadham High Street, offers a living history of one family's role as village blacksmith for 170 years. The forge is still in operation and can be seen in action most days it is open (mainly Friday to Sunday but phone ahead first). Telephone: 01279 843301.

Date walk completed:
....